"God shapes the world by prayer."

E. M. Bounds[1]

"Activity without prayer is pride
and prayer without activity
is presumption."

E. M. Bounds[2]

# What Should I Pray?

## My Personal Prayer Guide and Journal

*The weapons we fight with are not the weapons of the world.*
*On the contrary, they have divine power to demolish strongholds.*
*We demolish arguments and every pretension that sets itself up*
*against the knowledge of God, and we take captive*
*every thought to make it obedient to Christ.*
(2 Cor 10:4-5  NIV)

### Stephen H Berkey

GETWISDOM PUBLISHING

# Copyright

## Bible Translations Used:

# A Personal Message

In today's Christian life maintaining an effective prayer life can be difficult. Is your daily prayer time interrupted, frustrating, or do you become distracted? Do you wonder what to pray? This Prayer Guide has been designed to resolve these problems. It will improve, strengthen, encourage, and organize your prayer life. It is for people who struggle with their prayer life or those who want to boost or improve their daily time in prayer and want a more intimate relationship with God.

This Guide was born out of my own struggle with my morning prayer time which had dropped from an extended time every morning to 5-10 minutes on a good day. I successfully used this process to re-establish my own prayer life and you can too! You will know you have the ear of God because you will be guided to pray according to His Word. Your prayer time can take on eternal implications as you are guided on knowing what to pray.

The best thing about this book is that it is easy to use. Results can be achieved in a few days. I promise that if you follow the process in this Guide, you will look forward to your prayer time and begin to experience a new and growing relationship with God.

Take charge of your prayer life today, and watch your prayer time become effective and highly satisfying!

*Steve*

# Purpose of Prayer Guide

Several years ago I decided to reorganize my prayer time and create a systematic approach to praying over a month's time on the many different subjects I had scribbled down on scraps of note paper. The result was a prayer book that was useful to me. I organized the prayers I wanted to pray daily on several pages and then distributed all the other prayers over a 31-day period so that in any given month I would cover all the subjects and not feel bogged down each day with a long list of prayers that I could never complete. That was the inspiration for this Prayer Guide.

## 1.  What should I pray?
Many sample prayers are provided for each category and subject, and space is available for you to write your own prayer or notations.

## 2.  Provide resources for reference
In addition to the sample prayers there are 25 additional special reference subjects concerning prayer.

## 3.  Organize prayer materials
The Guide is organized in logical order with a detailed Table of Contents that allows you to find quickly what is needed. The material is usually presented in an outline format with a minimum of text and explanation so you can get to the meat of the topic. On the last page of the Introduction section is a page titled "How to Use Your Prayer Guide."

## 4.  Personalized prayer
Space is provided for you to write or outline your own prayers.

## 5.  Focus on prayer of eternal significance
The suggested prayers are based on scriptures that have eternal implications or consequences.

## 6.  What does the Bible say?
The Guide provides a structure for your prayer time and teaches what the Bible has to say about prayer. In addition, at the end of the Guide is a Bible study on "The Prayer of Jabez" from *The OBSCURE Bible Study Series*.

### 7. Encouragement

The Guide will help and encourage you through examples and sample prayers. It also provides sections on "Why Should I Pray?" and "Why Isn't Prayer Answered?" to help you understand what God expects when He calls you to pray.

### 8. Eliminate worrying about what to pray

There are many helpful examples you can use to guide your prayer time. The subject matter is broad and generally relevant for all types of users. The Guide also provides the lyrics to several songs that could be used in worship.

### 9. Reduce frustration with long lists of prayers on multiple subjects

This is the reason for the 31 Days of Prayer. My exceptionally long lists were one of the driving forces behind developing the original prayer book. I was frustrated with the lists of prayer concerns that I could never finish.

### 10. Reduce distractions

With this Guide you have all the material in one location and can focus on actually praying. You will be less likely to get distracted because you have structure and a path to travel through your prayer time.

### 11. Being consistent and accountable

The structure alone will be a great help in being consistent. Because you will not be praying the same prayers each day, your prayer time should not become repetitious. But the Guide cannot make you use it. It can only make the process easier, more enjoyable, and productive. In the end you are the one who must decide that you want to pray!

### 12. Help praying Scripture

The sample prayers use Scripture directly or indirectly or are based on Biblical concepts.

# Contents

## Resources

## Bible Study: Prayer of Jabez

# Introduction

## Why Should I Pray?

Communication is vital in all human relationships. It is just as vital in our relationship with God. God has chosen for us to communicate with Him through prayer, which allows us to develop and maintain intimacy with the Father. The Bible gives us many other practical reasons to pray:

**1. We are dependent on God to accomplish any good thing. Prayer is the key to our effectiveness.**

John 15:5     I am the vine; you are the branches. If a man remains in me and I in him, he will bear much fruit; apart from me you can do nothing. (NIV)

**2. We will learn great things.**

Jeremiah 33:3     Call to me and I will answer you and tell you great and unsearchable things you do not know. (NIV)

**3. We are protected from temptation.**

Matthew 26:41     Watch and pray so that you will not fall into temptation. The spirit is willing, but the body is weak. (NIV)

**4. Prayer is God's way for us to obtain our needs and desires. It is the key to His resources.**

Mt 7:7     Ask and it will be given to you; seek and you will find; knock and the door will be opened to you. (NIV)

Mt 18:19     Again I say to you, that if two of you agree on earth about anything that they may ask, it shall be done for them by my Father who is in heaven. (NIV)

**5. Prayer is the way we can overcome anxiety, worry, and fear.**

Psalm 34:4     I sought the LORD, and he answered me; he delivered me from all my fears. (NIV)

Philippians 4:6-7     Do not be anxious about anything, but in everything, by prayer and petition, with thanksgiving, present your requests to God. And the peace of God, which transcends all understanding, will guard your hearts and your minds in Christ Jesus. (NIV) [see also Lk 18:1]

**6. God asks us to pray.**

Luke 18:1     Then Jesus told his disciples a parable to show them that they should always pray and not give up. (NIV)

### 7. Prayer is a source of healing – it brings God's spiritual power.

James 5:16    Therefore confess your sins to each other and pray for each other so that you may be healed. The prayer of a righteous man is powerful and effective. (NIV)

### 8. Prayer is the key to revival.

2 Chronicles 7:14    If my people, who are called by my name, will humble themselves and pray and seek my face and turn from their wicked ways, then will I hear from heaven and will forgive their sin and heal the land. (NIV)

### 9. Prayer is essential to our relationship with God/Christ.

John 15:7    If you remain in me and my words remain in you, ask whatever you wish, and it will be given you. (NIV)

### 10. Prayer pleases God.

Pr 15:8    The LORD detests the sacrifice of the wicked, but the prayer of the upright pleases him. (NIV)

### 11. Because the devil is real.

1 Pet 5:8    Be self-controlled and alert. Your enemy the devil prowls around like a roaring lion looking for someone to devour. (NIV)

### 12. Jesus warns us to be alert and ready.

Luke 21:34    Watch out! Don't let your hearts be dulled by carousing and drunkenness, and by the worries of this life. Don't let that day catch you unaware. (NLT)

### 13. Prayer brings rescue.

Ps 109:31    For he stands at the right hand of the needy, to save him from those who condemn his soul to death. (ESV)

### 14. Prayer develops righteousness.

Ps 139:23-24    Search me, O God, and know my heart; test me and know my anxious thoughts. Point out anything in me that offends you, and lead me along the path of everlasting life. (NLT)

### 15. Jesus prayed.

This is reason enough! For this reason alone I will pray because if it was important to Jesus, then it should be important to me. Jesus' prayers are the topic for our next section.

# Jesus Prayed

We can conclude from the above that the practice of prayer is more than just the discipline of praying for ourselves and others. It is a lifestyle and attitude of yielding our lives to the will of God. The Bible tells us how to be effective in prayer, what to avoid, why to pray, and what to pray for. The Bible gives us three primary reasons to pray:

POWER
I am the vine; you are the branches. If a man remains in me and I in him, he will bear much fruit; apart from me you can do nothing. (John 15:5)
WISDOM
Call to me and I will answer you and tell you great and unsearchable things you do not know. (Jeremiah 33:3)
PROTECTION
Watch and pray so that you will not fall into temptation. The spirit is willing, but the body is weak. (Matthew 26:41)

For me the most compelling reason to pray is because Jesus prayed. If the all-powerful Son of God found it necessary and desirable to pray, then I should as well. Let's examine further what the Bible has to say about Jesus praying.

**1. Jesus needed to spend time alone with the Father.**
Jesus made the effort to find time alone with His Heavenly Father. He often withdrew when there were large crowds or when an important decision had to be made (such as before calling the disciples).

> Mark 1:35    Very early in the morning, while it was still dark, Jesus got up, left the house and went off to a solitary place, where he prayed. (NIV) [See also Lk 5:16; Lk 6:12; Mt 14:22-23.]

**2. Jesus prayed at a low point in His ministry and took disciples with Him when He withdrew to a mountain to pray.**

> Luke 9:28-29   About eight days after Jesus said this, he took Peter, John and James with him and went up onto a mountain to pray. As he was praying, the appearance of his face changed, and his clothes became as bright as a flash of lightning. (NIV)

### 3.  Jesus needed help in overcoming His own human will.

> Matt 26:39    Going a little farther, he fell with his face to the ground and prayed, "My Father, if it is possible, may this cup be taken from me. Yet not as I will, but as you will." (NIV)

### 4.  Jesus prayed about the future and put Himself in the hands of the Father.

> Luke 23:46  Jesus called out with a loud voice, "Father, into your hands I commit my spirit." When he had said this, he breathed his last. (NIV)

### 5.  Jesus prayed when He was criticized.
When Jesus was criticized for breaking the Sabbath rules (Lk 6:1-11), His reaction described in Luke 6:12 was to withdraw and pray.

### 6.  Jesus prayed for reassurance.

> Luke 9:18    Once when Jesus was praying in private and his disciples were with him, he asked them, "Who do the crowds say I am?" (NIV)

### 7.  Jesus prayed before every major decision or shift in ministry.

- Before deciding to travel into Galilee (Mk 1:35-39)
- Before choosing the Twelve (Lk 6:12-13)
- Before the crowds could make Him King (Jn 6:15)
- Before questioning the disciples about their belief (Lk 9:18)

### 8.  Jesus claimed again and again that He was doing His Father's will.
These scriptures seem to be examples of Jesus' obedience through powerful and constant prayer. [See Jn 5:19; 7:16; 8:28; 12:49; 15:15; 17:7.]

### 9.  Jesus spoke against ostentatious prayers. He wants us to be real in prayer.

> Mark 12:40    They [Pharisees] devour widows' houses and for a show make lengthy prayers. Such men will be punished most severely. (NIV)

# Conditions For Answered Prayer

## Why isn't prayer answered?

There are two traditional, and perhaps trite, responses to this question. The first is that God always *does* answer prayer – His answer may be "Yes," "No," or "Wait." The second is that God always *does* answer prayer – but not always in the way we're expecting, so we may not recognize His hand in the result. Although these responses may be true, they aren't always helpful, and they don't seem to get at the heart of the question.

## What are the conditions for answered prayer?

### Faith:
"Have faith in God," Jesus answered. "I tell you the truth, if anyone says to this mountain, 'Go, throw yourself into the sea,' and does not doubt in his heart but believes that what he says will happen, it will be done for him. Therefore I tell you, whatever you ask for in prayer, believe that you have received it, and it will be yours." (Mark 11:22-24 NIV)

### Pray according to His will:
. . . if we ask anything according to his will, he hears us. And if we know that he hears us – whatever we ask – we know that we have what we asked of him. (1 John 5:14-15 NIV)

### Obedience:
. . . receive from him anything we ask, because we obey his commands and do what pleases him. (1 Jn 3:22 NIV)

### Ask in Jesus' Name:
And I will do whatever you ask in my name . . . You may ask me for anything in my name, and I will do it. (John 14:13-14 NIV)

### Union with Christ and His teaching:
If you abide [remain] in Me, and My words abide [remain] in you, ask whatever you wish, and it shall be done for you. (John 15:7 NAS)

## Introduction

**Bear fruit:**
You did not choose me, but I chose you and appointed you to go and bear fruit – fruit that will last. Then the Father will give you whatever you ask in my name. (Jn 15:16 NIV)

## What are the hindrances to answered prayer?

**Unforgiven sin:**
We know that God does not listen to sinners. He listens to the godly man who does his will. (John 9:31 NIV)

**Pride:**
When you pray, do not be like the hypocrites, for they love to pray standing in the synagogues and on the street corners to be seen by men. (Mt 6:5 NIV)

**Wrong motives:**
When you ask, you do not receive, because you ask with wrong motives, that you may spend what you get on your pleasures. (James 4:3 NIV)

**Unresolved conflicts:**
When you stand praying, if you hold anything against anyone, forgive him, so that your Father in heaven may forgive you your sins. (Mark 11:25 NIV)

## Conclusion

The Bible says, in fact, commands, that we should pray. Luke 18 reports that Jesus told a parable about the need to persevere in prayer. In addition, Jesus prayed! But how and when God answers prayer is one of His great mysteries. He certainly has the power and right to answer or not answer prayer any time and in any way. We simply cannot dictate to Him how He's to answer! But the verses above seem to indicate that we may have a role in how and when God answers prayer.

There is also a certain spiritual and intimate aspect to prayer. It is just not about getting something we want; it's about communion with God. God has frequently changed my heart on some subject after I have talked with Him at length about it. He may even use me (or you) to be part of an answer.

You might look at the six "conditions" listed above and say, "If I need to be perfect for God to answer prayer, there is little chance He will answer my prayers." And to some extent there may be a grain of truth in that. I believe if we are in a state of continual and deliberate sin, God is not likely to answer our prayers until we deal with that sin.

You might conclude that these requirements are really nothing more than what we are each striving for on a daily basis. God knows that we are not perfect, but the closer we come to being in tune with His plan for our life, living in obedience, and serving Him by serving others, the more likely we are to influence God and unleash His power in our lives.

Some might argue that God has already made up His mind and we have little chance to impact some predetermined divine plan. Based on the Bible, that is simply not true. Many Biblical events were altered because of prayer. If God has no intention to be influenced, why would he urge us to pray? It would be an exercise in futility, and that is not in the nature of God.

# What Are Prayers of "Eternal Significance"?

A simple definition might be: *prayers that have important faith implications.* Another approach might be to say that the subjects of the prayers have a basis or foundation in scripture. They have some eternal implications, and are not about secular, temporal, or worldly needs.

For good examples of this type of prayer, consider the prayers of Paul throughout the New Testament. You can review Paul's prayers in the Resource material section of this book. For example:

> Col 1:9-11     For this reason, since the day we heard about you, we have not stopped praying for you and asking God to fill you with the knowledge of his will through all spiritual wisdom and understanding. And we pray this in order that you may live a life worthy of the Lord and may please him in every way: bearing fruit in every good work, growing in the knowledge of God, being strengthened with all power according to his glorious might so that you may have great endurance and patience . . . (NIV)

You might also pray for the Fruit of the Spirit (love, joy, peace, patience, kindness, goodness, faith, gentleness, self-control) to be manifested in your life. (Gal 5:22) Or you might pray for godly character:

1. HUMILITY: Give me a servant's heart.
2. ACCEPTABLE: Purify me so that I am acceptable in Your sight.
3. HOLY: Set me apart and empower me to act in a godly manner.
4. RIGHTEOUS: Allow me to know what is right and give me power to do it.
5. FAITHFUL: Help me stand firm and not waver in my faith.
6. JUST: Give me a heart for the oppressed. Teach me to act justly.
7. FORGIVING: Help me forgive as You forgave me.
8. COMPASSION: Give me a storehouse of love and compassion every day.
9. LOVE: Help me love You and my brothers with all my heart and soul.
10. WISDOM: Give me wisdom to know when I am not achieving the above.
11. POWER: Empower me to accomplish all of the above.

Praying the Scriptures is another option. For example, 1 John 1:9 in the NIV says: "If we confess our sins, he is faithful and just and will forgive us our sins and purify us from all unrighteousness." Therefore we might pray: *Forgive me, Lord, for my sins and cleanse me from all unrighteousness.*

# Facts to Remember About Prayer

1. DEFINITION: Prayer is simply talking with God. No special words or language is necessary.

2. WHAT/WHEN/WHERE: You can pray about anything, anytime, anyplace.

3. GOD HEARS: Scripture tells us that God _does_ hear our prayers and answers them.

4. POSITION: God will hear regardless of our physical position, however, kneeling signifies reverence and humiliation.

5. FAITH: Faith is vital in prayer. We must believe in Christ and believe He can answer our specific prayer requests.

6. ANSWERS: God may answer prayer in several ways: yes, no, maybe, wait.

7. QUID PRO QUO: We can't expect God to grant our requests if we are unwilling to accept and obey His requirements.

8. WORK: Because prayer can be difficult, patience and perseverance are needed.

9. FOCUS: When praying in a group, concentrate on talking to God, not on impressing others.

10. USE YOUR MIND: Use your mind when you pray. Don't just repeat meaningless phrases.

11. SPECIFIC: Be as specific as possible in your requests.

12. EXPECTANCY: Wait expectantly; watch and listen for His answers.

# How to Use Your Prayer Guide

There are six major sections to the Prayer Guide:

INTRODUCTION
Read this information about prayer initially and again as needed.

FOCUSED DAILY PRAYERS
Choose the subjects that interest you. These are prayer subjects you generally want to cover each day. You can choose to pray through the examples or use the space provided to outline or write out your own prayer.

31 DAYS OF PRAYERS
The prayer topics in this section generally have a long list of different subjects and it's likely you would never get through the list in any one prayer session. Therefore the topics are spread over 31 days so you can pray something different each day. Choose the subjects that interest you.

MY LIFE PRAYER
The purpose of this section is to examine your life values and goals in order to ultimately produce a brief Life Prayer. But the process itself will give you other very valuable information that can be the source of additional personal prayer.

RESOURCES
Scan and review this material so that you are aware of the content. The subjects are all listed on the Contents page. You may use this information a great deal or you may not need it very often. Use it as needed.

PRAYER OF JABEZ BIBLE STUDY
This is a lesson from Book 4 of *The OBSCURE Bible Study Series*. Answers to the discussion questions are provided at the end. It was designed as a group bible study so you might want to invite some friends and work through the questions. More details about the *OBSCURE* series can be found at:

**http://getwisdompublishing.com/products/**

SUMMARY – How to Proceed

1.  Familiarize yourself with the Prayer Guide.
    Review the purpose of the Prayer Guide (pp 6-7).
    Review the Table of Contents (pp 8-9).
    Read pages 20, 43, 107, and 117.

2.  Flip through the Focused Daily Prayers section.
    Choose the subjects that you initially want to use (maybe highlight).
    Where appropriate use the space to fill in names or prayer concerns.

3.  In the 31-Days section, find the day you will begin and choose the subjects that you want to cover in the next few weeks. You could pray through them all or just a few. You only will use the space for notes as needed.

### You're Ready!

4.  You can choose to pray the sample prayers provided or use the subjects to pray your own words.

5.  The sections on "My Life Prayer," "Resources," and the "Jabez Bible Study" can be used any time you are ready.

"When we pray, we align ourselves
with the purposes of God and
tap into the power of the Almighty."

David Jeremiah[3]

# Focused Daily Prayers

We all have certain prayers or prayer subjects we want to include in our daily prayers. These are subjects like worship, praise, thanksgiving, confession, forgiveness, repentance, and intercessory prayer. The Prayer Guide provides sample prayers and space to write, list, or outline your own prayer. I have also included the lyrics of several hymns. If you have your personal favorites, you could insert them at the appropriate location or copy them on the pages.

## Worship: Prayer for Effective Worship

May the nations praise you, O God. Yes, may all the nations praise you.
Let the whole world sing for joy. (Ps 67:3-4 NLT)

**PRAYER:**
Lord, I pray for a new and revived passion for worship in my life, and for Your presence to manifest itself in my worship. Lord Jesus, I want a seeking heart and a deep desire to know You in worship. Make Yourself known to me and give me an acute sensitivity to Your Spirit. I pray that all I do and say in worship will glorify and exalt Your Name; that Your Name will be magnified above all things great and small. Father, cleanse my heart, mind, and spirit, so that sin cannot interfere with my worship. I want an all-consuming hunger to know You in worship. Please eliminate distractions so that I can concentrate only on You.

_____
_____
_____
_____
_____
_____
_____
_____
_____
_____
_____
_____
_____

# Worship Songs

## Amazing Grace
John Newton

Amazing grace! How sweet the sound that saved a wretch like me!
I once was lost, but now am found;
Was blind, but now I see.

'Tis grace hath taught my heart to fear, And grace my fears relieved;
How precious did that grace appear
The hour I first believed!

Through many dangers, toils, and snares, I have already come;
'Tis grace that brought me safe thus far,
and grace will lead me home.

The Lord has promised good to me, His word my hope secures;
He will my shield and portion be,
as long as life endures.

When we've been there ten thousand years, Bright, shining as the sun
We've no less days to sing God's praise,
Than when we've first begun.

Amazing grace! How sweet the sound that saved a wretch like me!
I once was lost, but now am found,
Was blind, but now I see.

## Doxology

Praise God, from Whom all blessings flow;
Praise Him, all creatures here below;
Praise Him above, ye heavenly host;
Praise Father, Son, and Holy Ghost. Amen.

# How Great Thou Art!
### Carl Boberg

1. O Lord my God, when I in awesome wonder
Consider all the worlds Thy hands have made,
I see the stars, I hear the rolling thunder,
Thy power throughout the universe displayed,

Chorus:
Then sings my soul, my Savior God, to Thee;
How great Thou art, how great Thou art!
Then sings my soul, my Savior God, to Thee;
How great Thou art, how great Thou art!

2. When through the woods and forest glades I wander
And hear the birds sing sweetly in the trees;
When I look down from lofty mountain grandeur
And hear the brook and feel the gentle breeze, (Chorus)

3. And when I think that God, His Son not sparing,
Sent Him to die, I scarce can take it in;
That on the cross, my burden gladly bearing,
He bled and died to take away my sin; (Chorus)

4. When Christ shall come with shout of acclamation
And take me home, what joy shall fill my heart!
Then I shall bow in humble adoration
And there proclaim, my God, how great Thou art! (Chorus)

# Other Songs

There's Just Something About That Name, Gloria and Bill Gaither
Sweet Hour of Prayer, Wm. W. Walford
It is Well With My Soul, Horatio G. Spafford
I Need Thee Every Hour, A. Hawks and R. Lowry
Because He Lives, Gloria and Bill Gaither
Jesus, I Come, William T. Sleeper
I Love You Lord, Laurie Klein

# Praise and Thanksgiving

Lord God, I praise You! How majestic is Your Name! Your ways are loving and faithful. You are robed in holiness and majesty. Your greatness is too astounding to fathom. You come near to all who call on You. You fulfill the desires of those who love You. Let every creature praise Your holy Name.

I praise You, the heavens praise You, all the angels and the heavenly host praise You, for You are worthy of our praise. Let everything that has breath praise the LORD. Holy, Holy, Holy art Thou, O Lord. Amen

## Praise For His Attributes

| | | |
|---|---|---|
| His faithfulness | His trustworthiness | His truth/integrity |
| His power | His grace | His forgiveness |
| His goodness | His justice | His love |
| His mercy | His righteousness | His wisdom |

## Praise For What He Has Done

| | | |
|---|---|---|
| Our salvation | His indwelling Holy Spirit | His calling |
| His protection | His guidance | His teaching |
| His relationship | His blessings | His healing |
| Our adoption | His victory over Satan | His sealing |

_____
_____
_____
_____
_____
_____
_____
_____
_____
_____
_____
_____
_____
_____
_____
_____
_____
_____

## Praise Subjects

- My One and Only God (Is 45:5)
- My Almighty God (Ps. 89:8)
- My Loving God (I Jn. 4:16)
- My God of Justice (Ro. 3:26)
- My Faithful God (Dt. 7:9)
- My Mercy (Neh. 9:31)
- My Refuge/Protector (Ps. 62:7)
- My Holy God (Rev 4:8)
- My Personal God (Mt. 8:11)
- My Provider God (2 Cor. 9:8)
- My Shepherd (Ps. 23:1-3)
- My Peace (Ro. 16:20)
- My Healer (Ex. 15:26)
- My Comfort (2 Cor. 1:3)
- My Great Forgiver (Neh 9:17)
- My Burden Bearer (Ps. 68:19)
- My Encourager (Ps 3:3)
- My God of Joy (Ps. 21:6)

## Thanksgiving For His Gifts

- of eternal life
- of the indwelling Holy Spirit
- of forgiveness
- of being heirs to the Kingdom
- of God's grace
- of His love
- of salvation
- of a place in Heaven with Him
- of His Word
- of His mercy and compassion
- of the riches of Christ
- of power
- of free access to His throne
- of the church
- of freedom
- of peace
- of comfort
- of deliverance
- of reconciliation
- of hope
- of righteousness
- of His Son
- of our faith

# Confession: Sin and Idols

**Prayer:** Father God, enable me to deal with the idolatrous loves in my life and to remove them from influencing my behavior. Grant me the grace to accomplish this in my life. I pray that the Holy Spirit would bring about deep conviction concerning the sin and improper idols in my life.

## Idols

| | | | |
|---|---|---|---|
| Money | Self | Approval | Control |
| Pleasure | Food | Sleep | Darkness |
| Cursing | Abundance | The World | Possessions |

_____
_____
_____
_____
_____
_____
_____
_____
_____
_____
_____
_____
_____
_____
_____
_____
_____
_____
_____
_____
_____
_____
_____
_____

# Forgiveness and Repentance

**Prayer:** For the sake of Your name, O Lord, forgive my sins and trespasses, though they are great. I pray against the desire to do whatever I wish whenever I wish. Rather, I pray for freedom to do what I know I should do. Guide and direct me in Your ways. Cleanse my heart, open my mind, and do not allow sin to rule in my life.

# Personal Character

**Fruit of the Spirit:** Lord, fill me with Your character so that I demonstrate love, joy, peace, patience, kindness, goodness, faithfulness, gentleness, and self-control in my life.

_____
_____
_____
_____
_____
_____
_____

**Obedience:** Lord Jesus, help me to be obedient as You were obedient until death. Cause me to have a deep desire and ability to walk in Your ways. Enable me to overcome my rebellious spirit and submit to You in humble obedience. Allow Your love to abound in me more and more in knowledge and depth of understanding so that I may discern and know Your ways.

_____
_____
_____
_____
_____
_____
_____

**Thought Life:** Lord God, set my heart and mind on things above, not on worldly things. I want to fix my thoughts on Jesus and things of eternal importance, not earthly wants and desires. Transform me into Your likeness, and conform me to Your ways.

_____
_____
_____
_____
_____
_____
_____

**Speech:** Lord, guard my lips so that my speech is truthful, uplifting, caring, and encouraging. Help me hold my tongue when I have nothing worthwhile to say. Keep my lips from lies, from being boastful, from spreading gossip, and being deceitful. Lord, guard my lips against using bad language, from swearing, or using Your name in vain. Rather, enable me to praise and proclaim Your Name. Lord, help me admit error when I have spoken wrongly and enable me to think before I speak. Help me glorify You with all I say.

_____
_____
_____
_____
_____
_____
_____
_____
_____
_____
_____
_____
_____
_____
_____
_____
_____
_____
_____
_____
_____
_____
_____
_____
_____
_____
_____
_____
_____
_____
_____

# INTERCESSION: Praying For My Spouse

Instruction: Fill in your spouse's name and the appropriate "his/her" pronoun.


## For Your Spouse

- Jesus, work in and through _____ and lead _____ to be the kind of person that will glorify You in all _____ says and does.

- Jesus, keep _____'s heart right with You and teach _____ how to serve You in our family.

- Jesus, give _____ clarity of mind; thoughts that will build _____ up and encourage those around _____.

- Jesus, help _____ understand Your will for _____ life.

- Jesus, bless _____ and pour out your blessing on _____ in all areas of _____ life.


## For Yourself, Relative to Spouse

- Holy Spirit, empower me to do and say the things that will lift up, edify, and encourage my spouse.

- Father, I put all existing conflicts and differences, as well as all potential areas of conflict, at the foot of the cross.

- Lord God, change me so that my mind and heart are aligned with Your desires and plans for our family.

- I pray for a humble and forgiving spirit to saturate our family life. I pray that forgiveness would engulf us like a cloud.

- I pray that our home would be a place of peace, love, and respect; that we would think of each other's needs before our own.

Special prayer for our relationship and marriage:

_____
_____
_____
_____
_____
_____
_____
_____
_____
_____
_____
_____
_____
_____
_____
_____
_____
_____
_____
_____
_____
_____
_____
_____
_____
_____
_____
_____
_____
_____
_____
_____
_____
_____
_____
_____
_____
_____

# INTERCESSION: Praying For Children and Students

**My Children:**

_____

_____

_____

_____

_____

_____

_____

_____

_____

_____

_____

_____

_____

_____

_____

_____

_____

_____

_____

_____

_____

_____

_____

_____

_____

_____

_____

_____

_____

_____

_____

_____

_____

_____

_____

_____

_____

**Children and Students in General:**

**GENERAL:** I pray for a mighty work of God to transform the spiritual condition of our families. Lord Jesus, do a new thing among us and cause our families to be beacons to those who need to hear and see the love of Christ lived out among the family of God. May peace reign in our home. Amen.

**LOVE:** May our children/students experience Your love in authentic ways through the Christians they know. (Jn 13:35)

**PEACE:** May the peace that surpasses all understanding rule the hearts and minds of our children and every student, teacher, and administrator in our schools.

**TRUTH:** Release truth in our family and in our schools. Help students to discern truth and not believe false teaching. (Pr 23:23)

**PARENTS:** Give us the ability to discipline our children with love. Turn the hearts of the parents toward their children. (Dt 6:7; Mal 4:6; Eph 6:4)

**VIOLENCE:** Lord, protect our children and schools from violence. Protect all the students and the staff of our schools. Destroy any intent to harm our children. Expose any weapons brought on school premises and render them harmless. (Ps 34:7; 57:1)

**EVIL:** I pray that any evil that would deceive the minds of children into practicing any form of witchcraft or divination be made harmless. (Isa 8:19-20; Micah 5:12)

**SEXUAL PURITY:** May all students in our schools honor their sexuality and commit to sexual abstinence until marriage. Give each one the grace, strength, and courage required to live out this commitment. (1 Thes 4:3-5)

**ABORTION / DRUGS:** May our children and the students in our schools embrace the sanctity of human life. Heal any student or teacher from the addictive power of drugs or alcohol. Heal anyone who has experienced the pain of these evils. (Ps 139:13-16; 37:32-33)

**WITNESS:** Grant Christian students boldness in living and sharing the good news of their faith. (1Tim 4:12)

# INTERCESSION: Praying for the Lost

List the people you want to pray for on the next page
and mentally insert their names in the blanks below.

**CONVICT:** Father, I pray that You would convict _____, who is lost and separated from God. (Ro 3:23)

**DRAW:** Father, in the name of Jesus, I pray that You will draw _____ to Jesus, resulting in true faith and repentance. (Jn 6:44)

**FAITH:** Father, I pray that You would provide _____ with genuine saving faith; faith that trusts in Jesus alone as Savior. (Eph 2:8-10)

**FALSE TEACHING:** Father, in the name of Jesus, I pray that You would destroy any false thinking that _____ has about Jesus Christ. Reveal to _____ the truth about salvation. (Pr 14:12)

**GOSPEL:** Father, I pray that You will open _____'s heart and mind to understand, believe, and receive the gospel. (Acts 16:14)

**LIGHT:** Father, I pray that You will remove _____ from the kingdom of darkness and place _____ into the kingdom of light. (Col 1:13)

**MESSENGER:** Father, I pray that You will send harvesters into _____'s life until _____ receives and accepts the gospel. (Ro 10:14)

**SALVATION:** Father, I pray that _____ will receive the free gift of eternal life through Jesus Christ. (Romans 6:23)

**SATAN:** Father, destroy Satan's work in _____'s life and open _____ eyes to the truth of the good news of Jesus Christ. (2 Cor 4:4)

**SIN:** Father, I pray that You will cause _____ to reject sin and that You will break the bondage of the sins that are hindering _____ from coming to Christ. (Mark 9:43-47)

**SURRENDER:** Father, I ask that _____ would surrender to the Lord Jesus Christ (Ro 14:9), take up the cross, and follow You. (Luke 9:23)

**TRUST:** Father, I ask that _____ will not trust in in the world, but will completely trust in Jesus as Savior and Lord. (Gal 2:16)

**WORD:** Father, I pray that the Word will take root in _____'s life and bring true redemption. (Mt 13:6, 20-21)

_____

_____

_____

_____

_____

_____

_____

_____

_____

_____

_____

_____

_____

_____

_____

_____

_____

_____

_____

_____

_____

_____

_____

_____

_____

_____

_____

_____

_____

_____

## INTERCESSION: For Family, Friends, Others, Events, Church, etc.

**Daily Prayer**

"Remember, the shortest distance between a problem and the solution is the distance between our knees and the floor."

Charles Stanley[4]

# 31 Days of Prayer

Most of the prayers in this 31-day calendar are different than those provided in the Focused Prayer section above. These prayers are divided into the same eight categories for each day. You can choose to read the prayer, meditate on it, or pray your own words based on the focus of the prayer. You can also write out your own prayers in the space provided.

_The key here is to do what works for you._ If you are not sure what to pray, you can rely more on the sample prayers provided. Make it work for you.

You can pray on these subjects as much or as little as you prefer. There is no reason you have to pray through all the subjects at any particular time. You could choose to spend all your allotted time on just one subject. Again, make it work for you.

## A Prayer to Begin the Day

Lord, as today begins, I desire Your holiness and righteousness. Surround my heart and mind with Your love, contentment, wisdom, and faithful presence in my life.

Lord, I recognize Your power over all that I will think, speak, and do today. I thank You for Your many blessings in my life and I commit to honoring You in my family, work, and community. Give me strength, power, and wisdom to perform my duties. Saturate my performance with Your perspective and presence so that I honor You in all that I do and say today.

Lord, when I am at a loss or confused, enlighten my heart and mind. If I am frustrated, weary, or exhausted, empower me with Your Spirit. May my speech and activities bring satisfaction, encouragement, and joy to all those around me.

Lord, bless my family in all their plans and activities today. Protect them from evil. Bring peace, contentment, and rest into my home tonight as evening comes. Lord, thank You for what you are going to do in my life today and I give you thanks and praise for it. Amen.

# Day 1

**MY GOAL:**
Lord, I want You to be the central focus of my life.

**MY PRAISE:**
CREATOR: Creator God, I praise You because You made the heavens, even the highest heavens, and all their starry host, the earth and all that is on it, the seas and all that is in them. You give life to everything, and the multitudes of heaven worship You. (Neh. 9:6)

**MY THANKS:**
GRACE: I thank You, Lord, for the riches of Your grace that You have lavished on me in Christ Jesus.

**MY NEIGHBOR: Love One Another**
Purify me in Your truth so that I have sincere love for my brothers. Help me love those around me. (1 Peter 1:22; 1 John 4:7)

**MY COMMITMENT: To Relationship**
Lord Jesus, fill me with the power of truth so that I can have a growing personal relationship with You.

**FAMILY:**
PRESENCE: I pray that the Holy Spirit would saturate this community with His presence so that no family would be left untouched.

**MY LEADERS:** (general, world, country, local, church, business)
**General:** Lord, I pray that our leaders would fear God and recognize that they are accountable to God for each decision they make. (Pr 9:10)
**Pastor:** Father, I ask You to make Pastor _____ a person after Your own heart, one who will do Your will. (Acts 13:22; 1 Samuel 16:7)

**MY HOPE: Shamgar**
I want to be **fearless** like Shamgar, who picked up his oxgoad [farm implement] and killed 600 Philistines in defense of his faith and country.

> **Question:** Lord, what tool do You want me to pick up?

> **Prayer:** Lord, help me use the tools You gave me.

Journal your thoughts, make notes, or write your personal prayer:

_____
_____
_____
_____
_____
_____
_____
_____
_____
_____
_____
_____
_____
_____
_____
_____
_____
_____
_____
_____
_____
_____
_____
_____
_____
_____
_____
_____
_____
_____
_____
_____
_____
_____
_____
_____
_____
_____
_____
_____

## Day 2

**MY GOAL**
I want to be overwhelmed by the greatness of God.

**MY PRAISE:**
ONLY GOD: God, I praise You because You are the Lord, and there is no other; apart from You there is no God. (Is. 45:5)

**MY THANKS:** Father, I thank You for Jesus and His atoning sacrifice for me.

**MY NEIGHBOR:** Help me follow Your commandment to honor one another. (Ro 12:10b)

**MY COMMITMENT: To be a Living Sacrifice**
Lord Jesus, I offer my life to You as a living sacrifice. I pray that it is holy and pleasing to You. This is my spiritual act of worship. I do not want to conform to the pattern of this world, but to be transformed by the renewing of my mind so that I will know Your will for my life. (Ro 12:1-2)

**MY FAMILY:**
LOVE: I pray that my home and family would be filled with the love of God.

**MY LEADERS:** (world, country, local, church, business)
**General:** Lord, I pray that our leaders would have wisdom, knowledge, and understanding of Your ways. (James 1:5)
**Pastor:** Father, cause Pastor _____ to love the Word of God with all _____ heart and enable _____ to meditate on it daily. (Psalm 119:97) I ask that _____ would have the time and the discipline to study and understand Your Word. (1 Tim 4:15)

**MY HOPE: Benaiah**
I want the **courage** of Benaiah, who went into a pit on a snowy day to kill a lion and later struck down an Egyptian with his own spear.

> **Question**: Lord, what act of courage or bravery do You want me to perform?

> **Question**: Lord, what courageous decision do I need to make?

Journal your thoughts, make notes, or write your personal prayer:

## Day 3

**MY GOAL:** I want a white-hot passion for You.

**MY PRAISE:**
ALMIGHTY GOD: O Lord God Almighty, who is like You? You are mighty, O Lord; Your faithfulness surrounds You. (Ps. 89:8)

**MY THANKS:**
CHURCH: I thank You for the church; for its support and encouragement.

**MY NEIGHBOR:** Help me to honor Your command to be devoted to one another. (Ro 12:10b)

**MY COMMITMENT:**
AVAILABILITY: Lord, I want to be available when You want to use me for the work of the Kingdom. Prepare and equip me for Your service.

**MY FAMILY:**
FORGIVENESS: I pray Your forgiveness and blessing on my home and family.

**MY LEADERS:** (world, country, local, church, business)
**General:** Lord, I pray that unbelieving leaders would be presented with the Gospel in a loving Christian witness. (Ro 10:14-15) I pray that they would be drawn to a saving encounter with Christ, be born again, and be encouraged in their faith. (1 Tim 2:4; Eph 1:17-23)
**Pastor:** O Lord, I pray that You will guide Pastor _____ in all that _____ says and does. (Psalm 37:23)

**MY HOPE: Stephen.**
I want to **stand firm** like Stephen (a man full of grace), who was stoned to death for his **unwavering faith** and yet was able to say, "Lord do not hold this sin against them."

    **Question:** Lord, in what area in my life do I need to stand firm?

    **Question:** Lord, how can I help someone else stand firm?

Journal your thoughts, make notes, or write your personal prayer:

## Day 4

**MY GOAL:** I want my heart, mind, and soul to be occupied with God.

**MY PRAISE:**
ETERNAL GOD: I praise You, Lord, as the Ancient of Days (Dan. 7:9), the Everlasting Father (Is. 9:6) who lives forever and ever.

**MY THANKS:**
GOODNESS: I thank You, Lord, for Your great goodness and kindness.

**MY NEIGHBOR:** Help me to live in harmony with others. (Ro 12:16)

**MY COMMITMENT: To Praise**
Lord, help me offer You a continual sacrifice of praise. You are worthy of worship and praise. I want to glorify You every day in everything I do and say. I want my heart, mind, and soul to be thirsty for the Living God.

**MY FAMILY:**
BIBLICAL FAMILY: I pray for a Biblical approach to the roles of husband and wife and parenting.

**MY LEADERS:** (world, country, local, church, business)
**General:** Lord, I pray that our leaders would recognize their own inadequacy; that they would pray and seek Your will (Prov 3:5-8; Lk 11:9-13); that they would be convicted of sin (Ps 51:17; Jn 8:9), and seek to correct any wrongs they have caused.
**Pastor:** Father, make Pastor _____ into a mighty man/woman of prayer. (Mark 1:35)

**MY HOPE: Rizpah**
I want the **commitment**, **love**, and **dedication** of Rizpah who spent weeks (night and day) protecting the bodies of her dead family.

> **Question**: Lord, is there someone in my family who needs to be honored?

> **Question**: Lord, is there someone in my life who requires my full attention?

Journal your thoughts, make notes, or write your personal prayer:

_____
_____
_____
_____
_____
_____
_____
_____
_____
_____
_____
_____
_____
_____
_____
_____
_____
_____
_____
_____
_____
_____
_____
_____
_____
_____
_____
_____
_____
_____
_____
_____
_____
_____
_____
_____
_____
_____

## Day 5

**MY GOAL:** I want my being to be saturated with Your presence.

**MY PRAISE:**
LOVING GOD: I praise You because You are a loving God, whose very nature is love. (I Jn. 4:16)

**MY THANKS:**
EVIDENCE: I thank You, Father, that we can observe the evidence of Your attributes and character in Your creation.

**MY NEIGHBOR: Do Not Judge One Another**
Let us cease passing judgment on one another. Prevent me from putting any stumbling block or obstacle in my brother's way. (Ro 14:13)

**MY COMMITMENT: To Spiritual Sacrifices**
Dear God, allow me to offer spiritual sacrifices that honor and exalt Your Name. I pray that through prayer, worship, repentance, and self-denying service to Christ, I can live a life worthy of a child of God. (1 Peter 2:5)

**MY FAMILY:**
LOVE and FORGIVENESS: I pray that I and other parents will walk in love and demonstrate forgiveness to one another.

**MY LEADERS:** (world, country, local, church, business)
**General:** Lord, I pray that our leaders would read the Bible and seek answers from the Word of God; that they would attend Bible studies and grow in their knowledge of the Word. (Ps 119:11; Col 3:2)
**Pastor:** Father, I ask that You would continually enable, guide, and empower Pastor _____ in _____ Christian life and the ministry You have given _____. (Ephesians 5:18)

**MY HOPE: Hosea**
I want to be **obedient** like Hosea, who married the prostitute Gomer to illustrate to the Israelite people their unfaithfulness to God.

> **Prayer:** Lord, show me any areas of my life in which I'm being spiritually promiscuous.

Journal your thoughts, make notes, or write your personal prayer:

_____
_____
_____
_____
_____
_____
_____
_____
_____
_____
_____
_____
_____
_____
_____
_____
_____
_____
_____
_____
_____
_____
_____
_____
_____
_____
_____
_____
_____
_____
_____
_____
_____
_____

## Day 6

**MY GOAL:** I want You constantly before me.

**MY PRAISE:**
JUSTICE: Lord, I praise You and magnify You, because You are just and You are the one who justifies those who have faith in Jesus. (Ro 3:26)

**MY THANKS:**
SPIRITUAL GIFTS: I thank You for the spiritual gifts You have given me and pray that You will encourage and empower me to use them in Your service.

**MY NEIGHBOR: Accept One Another**
Lord, help me accept others just as Christ accepted me. (Ro 15:7)

**MY COMMITMENT: To Love**
I want to love You completely: heart, mind, body, and soul. I ask for a transparent honesty before You. Holy Spirit, I want to live a life of love just as Christ loved me and gave Himself up for me as an offering and sacrifice to God. I want to imitate Christ, and to love my brother as myself. (Eph 5:2)

**MY FAMILY:**
MARRIAGE: I pray that commitment and trust will be strengthened between my spouse and me, and between all husbands and wives.

**MY LEADERS:** (world, country, local, church, business)
**General:** Lord, I pray that our leaders would value the Ten Commandments and the teachings of Christ. (Ps 19:7-11; Jn 8:31-32)
**Pastor:** Lord, I ask that the Fruit of the Spirit would be powerfully and clearly displayed in Pastor _____'s life. (Galatians 5:22-23)

**MY HOPE: Real Friends**
I want the **perseverance** of the four men who lowered their friend down through a roof to Jesus in order for their friend to be healed.

> **Question**: Lord, in what areas do I need to strengthen my faith?

> **Question**: Lord, is there someone in my life who needs hope?

Journal your thoughts, make notes, or write your personal prayer:

## Day 7

**MY GOAL:** I want You to be foremost in my thoughts.

**MY PRAISE:**
FAITHFUL GOD: Father, I give You my praise and adoration. You are a faithful God, keeping Your covenant of love to a thousand generations. (Dt. 7:9)

**MY THANKS:**
FREEDOM: I thank You, God, that although I used to be a slave to sin, I know wholeheartedly that if I follow Your Word, I am free. (Ro:17-18)

**MY NEIGHBOR: Pray for One Another**
Therefore, confess your sins to one another and pray for one another, that you may be healed. The prayer of a righteous person has great power as it is working. (James 5:16 ESV)

**MY COMMITMENT: To Faith and Unity**
RIGHTEOUSNESS: Allow my faith to be a pleasing sacrifice that is the result of righteous living. May it be seen by others in order to glorify You. (Php 2:17)
UNITY: I pray for unity among the people of God. I pray that the church will have no divisions that hinder the plan of God. (1 Cor 1:10)

**MY FAMILY:**
RESTORATION: I pray for all those in my family who have strayed from God's path and need Your power and guidance to return to You.

**MY LEADERS:** (world, country, local, church, business)
**General:** Lord, I pray that our leaders would respect and honor their parents, setting an example for others. (Eph 6:2-3)
**Pastor:** Father, I ask that Pastor _____ will be humble, depending totally on You so _____ may be used by You. (1 Peter 5:5-6)

**MY HOPE: Queen Esther**
I want to **trust** in the Lord like Queen Esther who approached the King without permission in order to save her people, saying "If I perish, I perish."

> **Question:** Lord, am I waging any battles I cannot win?
> **Prayer:** Lord, help me discern others' motives and make wise choices.

Journal your thoughts, make notes, or write your personal prayer:

_____
_____
_____
_____
_____
_____
_____
_____
_____
_____
_____
_____
_____
_____
_____
_____
_____
_____
_____
_____
_____
_____
_____
_____
_____
_____
_____
_____
_____
_____
_____
_____
_____
_____
_____
_____

## Day 8

**MY GOAL:** I want the will and power to exalt and proclaim Your Name.

**MY PRAISE:**
MERCIFUL GOD: You are a gracious and merciful God (Neh. 9:31), and I praise You for Your great mercy.

**MY THANKS:**
TRANSFORMATION: I thank You for changing and transforming my life. Please continue Your good work in me.

**MY NEIGHBOR: Serve One Another**
Lord, help me serve my neighbors in love. (Gal 5:13)

**MY COMMITMENT: To Mercy and Compassion**
Search my heart, O God, and remove all selfishness and pride. Fill me with mercy and compassion. (Mt 12:7)

**MY FAMILY: Spiritual Awakening**
I pray that there will be a spiritual awakening in the families of this community that would transform the world!

**LEADERS:** (world, country, local, church, business)
**General:** Lord, I pray that our leaders would respect authority and practice accountability. (Ro 13:1-7)
**Pastor:** God, I pray that You would continue to make Pastor
_____ into a holy and godly person that You can use in a mighty and dynamic way. (1 Timothy 4:7, 6:11; Hebrews 12:14)

**MY HOPE: Disciples on Emmaus Road**
I want to be like these disciples whose **hearts were burning** within them while they were talking to Jesus.

> **Question:** Lord, are you walking along the road with me and I don't recognize Your presence?

> **Question:** Lord, is there someone to whom I need to explain the scriptures?

Journal your thoughts, make notes, or write your personal prayer:

_____

_____

_____

_____

_____

_____

_____

_____

_____

_____

_____

_____

_____

_____

_____

_____

_____

_____

_____

_____

_____

_____

_____

_____

_____

_____

_____

_____

_____

_____

_____

_____

_____

_____

_____

_____

_____

_____

## Day 9

**MY GOAL:** I want to constantly rejoice and be glad in You.

**MY PRAISE:**
REFUGE: I praise You, Lord, for You are my mighty rock, my refuge. (Ps. 62:7)

**MY THANKS:**
FAMILY: I thank You for the gift of my family and pray that Your blessing will fall on them.

**MY NEIGHBOR: Be Patient With One Another**
Lord, I want to be completely humble, gentle, and patient, bearing with others in love. (Eph 4:2-3)

**MY COMMITMENT: To the Word**
I pray for an all-consuming hunger to read, understand, and live the Word of God in my life.

**MY FAMILY:**
AWAKENING: Father, I pray for a mighty work of your Holy Spirit to transform the spiritual condition of my immediate and extended family. I pray for awakening, renewal, and revival in our families.

**MY LEADERS:** (world, country, local, church, business)
**General:** I pray that our leaders would have godly counsel and God-fearing advisors (Pr 24:6); that they would reject all counsel that violates the spiritual principles of God's Word.
**Pastor:** Father, enable Pastor _____ to overcome temptation and give _____ a hatred of sin in any form. (1 Cor 10:13)

**MY HOPE: Philip**
I want to **seize opportunities** like Philip, who introduced the Ethiopian eunuch to the Gospel.

> **Question:** Lord, to whom can I be a Philip?

> **Question:** Lord, what opportunities am I missing? Help me recognize your divine appointments.

Journal your thoughts, make notes, or write your personal prayer:

## Day 10

**MY GOAL:** I want to forever delight in Your presence.

**MY PRAISE:**
PATIENCE and PERSEVERANCE: Father, I praise You because You are patient, not wanting anyone to perish, but everyone to come to repentance. Thank You for Your patience. (2 Peter 3:9)

**MY THANKS:**
LOVE: I thank You for the love that You have demonstrated to us in Your Son, who radiates Your glory and attests to Your faithfulness.

**MY NEIGHBOR: Forgive One Another**
Lord, help me to be kind, compassionate, and forgiving. (Eph 4:32)

**MY COMMITMENT: To Seeking You**
I want to seek You with all my heart and find You. Lord Jesus, I ask for a new fervency in seeking You in personal prayer.

**MY FAMILY:**
BEING LIGHT: Lord Jesus, do a new thing among us and cause my family to be beacons to those who need to hear and see the love of Christ being lived out among the family of God.

**MY LEADERS:** (world, country, local, church, business)
**General:** Lord, I pray that our leaders would be honest and faithful to their spouses and their families. (Mal 2:15-16)
**Pastor:** Lord, teach Pastor _____ the truth of the Word of God by the power of the Holy Spirit so that _____ can explain, proclaim, and defend the Word of God. (1 Timothy 3:1-7, 15; 1 Peter 5:1-4)

**MY HOPE: Jabez**
I want to have the **<u>boldness</u>** of Jabez who boldly prayed for God's blessing.

> **Question:** Lord, am I too passive in my prayers? Are my prayers big enough?

> **Question:** Lord, what life-changing things should I be praying for?

Journal your thoughts, make notes, or write your personal prayer:

## Day 11

**MY GOAL:** I want to glorify You in mind, body, and spirit.

**MY PRAISE:**
MY SAVIOR: I give praise to You, Father, the only God our Savior. To You be glory, majesty, power and authority, through Christ our Lord, before all ages, now and forevermore. (Jude 25)

**MY THANKS:**
ATONEMENT: Thank You, Jesus, for Your atoning sacrifice for me.

**MY NEIGHBOR: Submit to One Another**
Lord, help me to submit to others out of reverence for Christ. (Eph 5:21)

**MY COMMITMENT: To His Presence**
Change my heart, O God, so that I can fully experience Your presence.

**MY FAMILY:**
BEST I CAN BE: Lord, show me how to be the very best I can be. Help me to support my spouse and encourage my family.

**MY LEADERS:** (world, country, local, church, business)
**General:** Lord, I pray that our national leaders would regularly attend church and actively serve in ministry. (Heb 10:25)
**Pastor:** Father, I pray that You would give _____ a servant's heart and enable _____ to compassionately minister to our congregation and the lost in this community. (Philippians 2:5)

**MY HOPE: Elihu**
I want the **humility and patience** of Elihu, one of Job's friends, who waited to speak, allowing the elders to speak first, but was not shy to speak his mind.

> **Question:** Lord, do I need to work on my humility? Am I prideful?

> **Question:** Lord, what should I change in my life to be more humble?

Journal your thoughts, make notes, or write your personal prayer:

_____

_____

_____

_____

_____

_____

_____

_____

_____

_____

_____

_____

_____

_____

_____

_____

_____

_____

_____

_____

_____

_____

_____

_____

_____

_____

_____

_____

_____

_____

_____

_____

_____

_____

_____

_____

_____

_____

## Day 12

**MY GOAL:** I want always to uphold and display Your greatness.

**MY PRAISE:**
HOLINESS: Holy, holy, holy are You, Lord God Almighty, who was, and is, and is to come. (Rev 4:8)

**MY THANKS:** I give thanks, for your Name is near. (Ps 75:1)

**MY NEIGHBOR: Teach One Another**
Let the word of Christ dwell in me richly as we teach and admonish one another. (Col 3:16)

**MY COMMITMENT:**
TRUTH: Teach me to know right from wrong. I want to walk in the light, and be guided by Your Spirit.

**MY FAMILY:**
BUILD UP: Holy Spirit, empower me to do and say the things that will lift up and edify my spouse and children, and not tear them down.

**MY LEADERS:** (world, country, local, church, business)
**General:** Lord, I pray that our leaders would seek after purity, holiness, and righteousness. Help them to avoid sinful behavior. (1 Cor 6:9-20; Titus 2:12)
**Pastor:** I pray that You would create in Pastor _____ the faith that pleases You. Enable _____ to approach You, knowing that You reward those who diligently seek after You. (Heb 11:6)

**MY HOPE: Noah**
I want to be **all-in** like Noah, who built an ark for 100+ years, because God found him a righteous and blameless man. He walked in God's **grace**.

> **Question:** Lord, is there someone to whom I need to grant grace?

> **Prayer:** Lord, empower me to walk rightly that I, like Noah, may find favor in your eyes.

Journal your thoughts, make notes, or write your personal prayer:

## Day 13

**MY GOAL:** I want to saturate my life with the glory that surrounds You.

**MY PRAISE:**
PERSONAL GOD: I praise You, God, because You are a personal God, who gives me the honor of knowing You personally, even inviting me to feast at Your kingdom's table with Abraham, Isaac, and Jacob. (Mt. 8:11)

**MY THANKS:**
RECONCILIATION: I thank You for Your reconciling work in my life.

**MY NEIGHBOR: Encourage One Another**
Lord, help me to encourage others and build them up, to encourage others daily, and to consider how I may spur others on toward love and good deeds. (1 Thess 5:11; Heb 3:13)

**MY COMMITMENT: To Evangelism**
Holy Spirit, empower me to proclaim the Gospel so that Jews and Gentiles alike might become an offering acceptable to You. (Ro 15:16)

**MY FAMILY:**
CONFLICT: Father, I put all existing and potential areas of conflicts and differences in our family at the feet of Jesus.

**MY LEADERS:** (world, country, local, church, business)
**General:** I pray that leaders would be reliable and dependable.
(Mt 21: 28-31)
**Pastor:** I pray that Pastor _____ would be a Christ-centered and Christ-exalting preacher. (1 Corinthians 2:1-4)

**MY HOPE: Job**
I want a **relationship** with God like Job, whom God described as being a servant, blameless, fearing God, and shunning evil. Even in his suffering he did not sin.

> **Question:** Lord, help me trust You in all circumstances.

> **Question:** Lord, is there anyone who needs my help in their suffering?

Journal your thoughts, make notes, or write your personal prayer:

_____
_____
_____
_____
_____
_____
_____
_____
_____
_____
_____
_____
_____
_____
_____
_____
_____
_____
_____
_____
_____
_____
_____
_____
_____
_____
_____
_____
_____
_____
_____
_____
_____
_____

## Day 14

**MY GOAL:** I want to recognize the beauty and majesty of Your Creation.

**MY PRAISE:**
GENEROSITY: All praise and honor be Yours, O God. You are a generous God, who did not stop short of giving Your own Son.

**MY THANKS:**
CHURCH: I thank You for the church; for its support and encouragement.

**MY NEIGHBOR: Carry One Another's Burdens**
Help me carry the burdens of others, thus fulfilling the law of Christ.

**MY COMMITMENT: To Your Presence**
I pray that others will recognize Your presence in my life. Help me abide in Your love, grace, and wisdom.

**MY FAMILY:**
YOUR WILL: Lord God, change my desires so that they are aligned with Your desires and plans for my family.

**MY LEADERS:** (world, country, local, church, business)
**General:** Lord, I pray that our leaders would be honest in all financial matters and use the Word for a foundation on issues of ethics.
(1 Cor 6:10; 1 Tim 6: 6-10)
**Pastor:** Lord, I ask that Pastor _____ would be faithful in preaching all of the Word of God. (Acts 20:20-21)

**MY HOPE:  Daniel's Friends**
I want the **faith**, **commitment**, and **fortitude** of Daniel's friends who **stood firm**. They refused to bow down and worship a statue, even at the cost of being thrown into a fiery furnace.

> **Question:** Lord, where have I compromised any of my values?

> **Question:** Lord, where in my life do I need to take a stand?

Journal your thoughts, make notes, or write your personal prayer:

# Day 15

**MY GOAL:** I want to be overwhelmed by Your acts of power, Your mighty deeds, and Your surpassing greatness.

**MY PRAISE:**
PROVIDER: I praise You today, Lord, as my Jehovah-Jireh (the Lord Will Provide), who makes all grace abound in me and generously provides all I need. (2 Cor. 9:8)

**MY THANKS:**
YOUR CHARACTER: I thank You, Father, for the evidence we can observe of Your nature and character in Your creation, Your people, and Your attributes.

**MY NEIGHBOR: Be Humble Toward One Another**
Lord, help me clothe myself with humility toward others, because God opposes the proud but gives grace to the humble. (1 Peter 5:5)

**MY COMMITMENT: To Prayer**
Lord Jesus, I ask that my home and our church be true houses of prayer, so we can be renewed and empowered in Your service.

**MY FAMILY:**
PRAISE: Father, Jesus, Holy Spirit, I humbly ask that You would cause all we do as a family to glorify, honor, exalt, and magnify You.

**LEADERS:** (world, country, local, church, business)
**Pastor:** I pray that Pastor _____ would preach in the power and the will of the Holy Spirit. (Acts 4:8-12)

**MY HOPE: Ananias**
I want to be like Ananias, who **trusted and obeyed** Jesus in what appeared to be a very dangerous situation (going to pray for Saul/Paul).

> **Question:** Lord, in whose life do I need to be an Ananias?

> **Question:** Lord, in what situation do I need to trust and obey You?

Journal your thoughts, make notes, or write your personal prayer:

## Day 16

**MY GOAL:** I want to have a consuming passion for God.

**MY PRAISE:**
SHEPHERD: I bless Your name and praise You as my Jehovah-Rohi
(The Lord My Shepherd), who will shepherd and guide me in the paths of
righteousness for Your name's sake. (Ps. 23:1-3)

**MY THANKS:**
SKILLS: I thank You for the skills and abilities You have given me and I pray
that You will encourage and empower me to use them in Your service.

**MY NEIGHBOR: Do Not Slander One Another**
Lord, help me to remember not to slander others. (James 4:11)

**MY COMMITMENT: To Serving You**
Lord, encourage me to serve You with gladness in all things. May all I do be
done as unto Christ. Allow me to find joy in all tasks that serve others. Give
me the power to pick up the basin and the towel like Jesus. (John 13:5)

**MY FAMILY:**
GOD'S BLESSING: I pray that the Lord would bless this community with His
grace so that no family would be left unaffected.

**MY LEADERS:** (world, country, local, church, business)
**General:** Lord, I pray that our leaders would have teachable spirits. (Ro 1:21)
**Pastor:** I pray that the Word of God would be central and absolute in Pastor
_____'s preaching and ministry. (2 Timothy 3:15-16)

**MY HOPE:  Mary**
I want the **wisdom** of Mary (Jesus' mother) who told the servants at the
wedding in Cana to "do whatever He tells you."

   **Question:** Lord, in what area do I need to trust you more fully?

   **Prayer:** Lord, give me wisdom to see clearly how to serve you.

Journal your thoughts, make notes, or write your personal prayer:

_____
_____
_____
_____
_____
_____
_____
_____
_____
_____
_____
_____
_____
_____
_____
_____
_____
_____
_____
_____
_____
_____
_____
_____
_____
_____
_____
_____
_____
_____
_____
_____
_____
_____
_____
_____
_____
_____
_____

## Day 17

**MY GOAL:** I want constantly to live in submission to You.

**MY PRAISE:**
VICTORY: Praise to You, my God, because You are my Jehovah-Nissi (The Lord My Banner), God, my victory, who always leads me in triumphal procession in Christ. (2 Cor. 2:14)

**MY THANKS:**
OVERCOME: I thank you, God, that although I was formerly a slave to sin, You have given me the ability to overcome my sinful nature.

**MY NEIGHBOR: Spur One Another On**
Let me consider how I may spur others on toward love and good deeds. (Heb 10:24)

**MY COMMITMENT: To Uplifting Speech**
May my words be a blessing to You. Guard my tongue so that my speech is true and uplifting. Help me use words that are helpful, kind, and healing.

**MY FAMILY:**
LOVE: I pray that love would permeate our family: love for God and love for one another.

**MY LEADERS:** (world, country, local, church, business)
**General:** Lord, I pray that our leaders would have hearts full of mercy and compassion for the needy, poor, and unfortunate. (Lk 10:33-37)
**Pastor:** Lord, I pray that You would use Pastor _____'s preaching to save the lost, to mature the believers, and to build up Your church. (Ephesians 4:11-16; 2 Timothy 4:5)

**MY HOPE: 24 Elders**
I want to be able to **submit to the Lord Almighty and worship** like the 24 Elders who cast their crowns at the feet of Jesus.

   **Question:** Lord, how can I be better prepared to meet You in worship?
   **Question:** Lord, how can I make You my primary focus in worship?
   **Question:** Lord, am I doing anything unacceptable in worship?

Journal your thoughts, make notes, or write your personal prayer:

## Day 18

**MY GOAL:** I want constantly to seek after the heart of God.

**MY PRAISE:**
PEACE: I praise You with all my heart, Lord, because You are my Jehovah-Shalom (The Lord Our Peace), the God of peace who will soon crush Satan under my feet. (Ro. 16:20)

**MY THANKS:** I thank You for changing and transforming my life. Please continue Your good work in me.

**MY NEIGHBOR: Be Truthful To One Another**
Lord, I pray that I will stop all lies and speak truthfully to my neighbors.

**MY COMMITMENT: To Witness**
Lord Jesus, I ask for true change in the areas of my life that hinder my witness for the Gospel.

**MY FAMILY:**
FORGIVENESS: I ask for forgiveness to permeate every home in our community. Lord, make forgiveness the watchword in my family.

**MY LEADERS:** (world, country, local, church, business)
**General:** Lord, I pray that our leaders would have the courage to resist manipulation and compromise of godly principles. (Pr 29:25; 2 Tim 1:7)
**Pastor:** I ask that Pastor _____ be faithful in preaching Your truth in spite of any opposition or indifference. (1 Timothy 6:12, 20-21; 2 Timothy 3:13-14, 4:2-4)

**MY HOPE: Demas**
I want to be **loyal**. I do not want to be like Demas, who deserted Paul for the love of the world.

>    **Question:** Lord, how have the world's values impacted my faith?
>    **Question:** Lord, in what ways do I love the world too much?
>    **Prayer:** Lord, do not allow the world to influence my walk with You.

Journal your thoughts, make notes, or write your personal prayer:

_____

_____

_____

_____

_____

_____

_____

_____

_____

_____

_____

_____

_____

_____

_____

_____

_____

_____

_____

_____

_____

_____

_____

_____

_____

_____

_____

_____

_____

_____

_____

_____

_____

_____

_____

_____

_____

_____

## Day 19

**MY GOAL:** I want to experience Your joy in all I do.

**MY PRAISE:**
HEALING: I praise You because You are the Lord who heals me. (Ex. 15:26)

**MY THANKS:**
Thank You for the gift of Your Spirit. Thank You for working in my life.

**MY NEIGHBOR: Look to the Interests of One Another**
Lord, help me to look not only to my own interests, but also to the interests of others. (Phil 2:4)

**MY COMMITMENT: To Gratitude**
Help me to be grateful in all circumstances. Enable me to express gratitude and joy in any and every situation. Guard me from being a sluggard and halt my grumbling tongue and negative attitudes.

**MY FAMILY:**
JOY: I pray that our family would have fun and enjoyment in all we do. Bring happiness into our lives as a family so others can observe our joy in You.

**MY LEADERS:** (world, country, local, church, business)
**General:** Lord, I pray that the leaders of our country would restore the sanctity of life, divine order, and morality in our nation. (Eph 5:21-6:4)
**Pastor:** Enable Pastor _____ to intercede for and instruct our congregation according to Your will. (1 Sam 12:23; Ro 1:9-10)

**MY HOPE: Virgin Mary**
I want to be able to **submit** like Mary (Virgin Mary) who said, "I am the Lord's servant; may it be to me as you have said."

> **Question:** Lord, what area in my life have I not surrendered to You?
>
> **Question:** Lord, is there something I need to turn over to You?
>
> **Prayer:** Lord, give me the courage to obey Your instructions.

Journal your thoughts, make notes, or write your personal prayer:

_____

_____

_____

_____

_____

_____

_____

_____

_____

_____

_____

_____

_____

_____

_____

_____

_____

_____

_____

_____

_____

_____

_____

_____

_____

_____

_____

_____

_____

_____

_____

_____

_____

_____

_____

_____

## Day 20

**MY GOAL:** I want You to be the first thing I think about every morning and the last thing every night.

**MY PRAISE:**
COMFORT: Praise be to the God and Father of our Lord Jesus Christ, the Father of compassion and the God of all comfort. (2 Cor. 1:3)

**MY THANKS:**
JUSTICE and GRACE: I thank You for the justice that You have demonstrated to me in all Your works. I am most grateful for Your grace.

**MY CHARACTER:**
OBEDIENCE: Help me to be obedient as You were obedient until death. Cause me to have a deep desire to walk in Your ways.

**MY COMMITMENT: To Trusting You**
Lord, help me trust You completely in all things. I want to be surrendered to Your will in all aspects of my life.

**MY FAMILY:**
HOLINESS: I pray that all parents will walk in faith and love, and demonstrate forgiveness to one another. I pray we will walk holy as You are holy.

**MY LEADERS:**
**General:** Lord, I pray that our leaders would put the interests of our country ahead of their personal interests and gain; that they would reject the influence of those who would lead them astray and tempt them to violate the will of God.
**Pastor:** Enable Pastor _____ to equip the saints for service and discipleship. (Ephesians 4:11-12; 2 Timothy 2:12)

**MY HOPE: Isaiah**
I want to be **committed** like Isaiah, who said, "Here I am, send me." (Isa 6:8)

> **Question:** Lord, what commitments do you desire from me?

> **Prayer:** Lord, empower me to respond according to Your will.

Journal your thoughts, make notes, or write your personal prayer:

_____
_____
_____
_____
_____
_____
_____
_____
_____
_____
_____
_____
_____
_____
_____
_____
_____
_____
_____
_____
_____
_____
_____
_____
_____
_____
_____
_____
_____
_____
_____
_____
_____
_____
_____
_____
_____

## Day 21

**MY GOAL:** Lord, I want You to be the central and driving force in my life!

**MY PRAISE:**
MIRACLES: Lord, I praise You because You are the God who performs miracles. You display Your power among the peoples. (Ps 77:14)

**MY THANKS: For Eternal Life**
Lord, I am so thankful for the generous gift of Your Son, through whom You provided forgiveness of my sins and granted me eternal life!

**MY NEIGHBOR: Do Not Provoke One Another**
Lord, keep me from being conceited, and from provoking others. (Gal 5:26)

**MY COMMITMENT:**
HUMILITY: Empower me to walk humbly in the path You have set before me. Allow me to serve the needs of others and put their needs ahead of my own.

**MY FAMILY:**
TRUST: I pray that commitment and trust will be strengthened between my spouse and myself and all other husbands and wives.

**MY LEADERS:** (world, country, local, church, business)
**General:** Lord, I pray that our leaders would work against the force of humanism which attempts to elevate man over God.
**Pastor:** Father, I ask You to protect _____ from Satan and all his attacks. I also ask You to protect and strengthen _____ from attacks by church members. (2 Tim 4:15-18; 2 Cor 11:26)

**MY HOPE: Joanna and Susanna**
I want to be like Joanna and Susanna who **humbly and quietly provided help and support** to Jesus.

> **Question:** Lord, could I make a commitment like these women?

> **Prayer:** Lord, I need Your help to fully commit my time and resources to Your kingdom.

Journal your thoughts, make notes, or write your personal prayer:

_____

_____

_____

_____

_____

_____

_____

_____

_____

_____

_____

_____

_____

_____

_____

_____

_____

_____

_____

_____

_____

_____

_____

_____

_____

_____

_____

_____

_____

_____

_____

_____

_____

_____

_____

_____

_____

_____

_____

_____

## Day 22

**MY GOAL:** I want to be absolutely sold out to the Kingdom of God.

**MY PRAISE:**
FORGIVING GOD: You are a forgiving God, gracious and compassionate, slow to anger and abounding in love. (Neh 9:17)

**MY THANKS:**
GOODNESS AND MERCY: I give thanks to You, Lord, for You are good and Your love endures forever. (Ps 106:1)

**MY CHARACTER: Make Me Holy**
Make me holy as You are holy. Set me apart for Your work. Give me strength to walk in Your ways.

**MY COMMITMENT: To Righteousness**
Fill me with Your righteousness that I may be blameless in Your sight. Empower me to be right with You and with others.

**MY FAMILY:**
RELATIONSHIPS: I pray for reconciliation, healing, and restoration in families. Lord, protect my family from any evil that would destroy our relationships.

**MY LEADERS:** (world, country, local, church, business)
**General:** Lord, I pray that our leaders would be prepared to leave their office if it is in the best interest of our country.
**Pastor:** Lord, I ask You to give Pastor _____ insight and direction into the solutions for the problems of the church. (1 Kings 3:7-9)

**MY HOPE: Nehemiah**
I want to be **sold out** like Nehemiah, who wept, mourned, fasted, and prayed when he learned that the walls and gates of Jerusalem were broken down and burned. (Neh 1:3-4)

> **Question:** Lord, does it break my heart to see broken places in Your church?

> **Prayer:** Lord, give me the empathy and will to repair broken places!

Journal your thoughts, make notes, or write your personal prayer:

_____

_____

_____

_____

_____

_____

_____

_____

_____

_____

_____

_____

_____

_____

_____

_____

_____

_____

_____

_____

_____

_____

_____

_____

_____

_____

_____

_____

_____

_____

_____

_____

_____

_____

_____

_____

## Day 23

**MY GOAL:** I want an intensified awareness of the divine.

**MY PRAISE**
PROTECTION: Thank You, Lord, for being my protection, my shield, and my refuge in times of trouble.

**MY THANKS:**
HOLY SPIRIT: Thank You, Lord God, for the gift of Your Holy Spirit who seals and guarantees my salvation.

**MY CHARACTER:**
WISDOM: Lord God, allow Your wisdom and love to reside in me. Give me knowledge and deep insight that I may discern and know Your ways. Fill my life with knowledge and understanding so that I make wise choices.

**MY COMMITMENT: To the Fear of the Lord**
Lord, I will live in the fear of the Lord because it is the gateway to wisdom.

**MY FAMILY:**
PRAYER: Lord, help us to pray together as a family.

**MY LEADERS:** (world, country, local, church, business)
**General:** I pray that our leaders would continue or restore dignity, honor, trustworthiness and righteousness to the office in which they serve.
**Pastor:** God, give Pastor _____ wisdom and discernment in counseling those who seek help or advice. (Proverbs 2:6)

**MY HOPE: Zacchaeus**
I want to be **zealous** like Zacchaeus, who climbed a tree to see Jesus. (Lk 19:4)

> **Question:** Lord, how can I more aggressively seek You out?

> **Prayer:** Lord, help me persevere in knowing You.

Journal your thoughts, make notes, or write your personal prayer:

_____

_____

_____

_____

_____

_____

_____

_____

_____

_____

_____

_____

_____

_____

_____

_____

_____

_____

_____

_____

_____

_____

_____

_____

_____

_____

_____

_____

_____

_____

_____

_____

_____

_____

_____

_____

## Day 24

**MY GOAL:** I want a deep personal hunger for the truth of Your Word.

**MY PRAISE:**
FAITHFUL: I praise You because Your love reaches to the heavens and Your faithfulness to the skies. (Ps 36:5) Great is Your faithfulness. (Lm. 3:23)

**MY THANKS:**
GOODNESS: I give thanks to the Lord, for He is good. His steadfast love endures forever! (Ps 106:1 ESV)

**My CHARACTER: Do Not Waver**
Deepen my resolve and help me stand up against any pressure to waver in my beliefs. Allow my strong faith and will to be an example to others.

**MY COMMITMENT: To Your Will**
Fill me with Your power so my life will cause others to see You in me. Give me courage and trust to carry out Your will for my life.

**MY FAMILY:**
RENEWAL: Father, I pray for a mighty work of your Holy Spirit to transform the spiritual condition of my immediate and extended family. I pray for awakening, renewal, and revival in the families of my community.

**MY LEADERS:** (world, country, local, church, business)
**General:** Lord, I pray that our leaders would acknowledge God as Creator and be good stewards of our environment.
**Pastor:** I pray that Pastor _____ would have a strong, close, harmonious relationship with those in leadership in our church.

**MY HOPE: Jesus**
I want to have a **servant's heart** and **humility** like Jesus, who washed the feet of His disciples and told them to wash one another's feet. (Jn 13:1-17)

> **Question:** Lord, am I humbly walking with my God? (Micah 6:8)

> **Question:** Lord, how can I humbly serve others?

> **Prayer:** Lord, help me put the needs of others before my own.

Journal your thoughts, make notes, or write your personal prayer:

_____
_____
_____
_____
_____
_____
_____
_____
_____
_____
_____
_____
_____
_____
_____
_____
_____
_____
_____
_____
_____
_____
_____
_____
_____
_____
_____
_____
_____
_____
_____
_____
_____
_____
_____
_____

## Day 25

**MY GOAL:** I want a genuine relationship and deep connection with Jesus.

**MY PRAISE:**
KING: All honor and praise be to You, my God, the blessed and only Ruler, the King of kings and Lord of lords, who alone is immortal and who lives in unapproachable light. (1Tim. 6:15)

**MY THANKS:**
REIGN IN POWER: Thank You for the example of the 24 elders who worship and give thanks continually because the Lord Almighty reigns in power.

### My NEIGHBOR: Exhort One Another
Lord, help me exhort others so that we are not hardened by the deceitfulness of sin. (Heb 3:13)

### MY COMMITMENT: To Obedience
Lord, I acknowledge my ineffective and rebellious response to Your commandments. Help me to love Your instructions and abide in Your Word.

**MY FAMILY:**
BEACONS: Lord Jesus, do a new thing among us and cause my family to be a beacon to those who need to hear and see the love of Christ lived out.

**MY LEADERS:** (world, country, local, church, business)
**Pastor:** Father, I ask that Pastor _____ be empowered to respond to any criticism in a gracious and Christ-like way, being faithful to God and His Word. (Mt 5:10-12, 43-48, 10:28; Ro 12:14, 17-21)

### MY HOPE: Paul
I want to live in **submission** to Christ, like Paul, who considered himself a slave of Jesus. (Php 1:1)

      **Question:** Lord, am I living in true submission?

      **Question:** In what ways can I trust and depend on You more?

      **Question**: Lord, am I a true disciple? How does my life show that?

Journal your thoughts, make notes, or write your personal prayer:

_____
_____
_____
_____
_____
_____
_____
_____
_____
_____
_____
_____
_____
_____
_____
_____
_____
_____
_____
_____
_____
_____
_____
_____
_____
_____
_____
_____
_____
_____
_____
_____
_____
_____
_____
_____
_____
_____
_____

## Day 26

**MY GOAL:** I want Christ to be the centerpiece of my life.

**MY PRAISE:**
DELIVERER: I praise You because You are my help and my deliverer. (Ps 70:5)

**MY THANKS:**
CHURCH: I thank God for all those churches that are demonstrating their faith, exhibiting their love, and providing evidence of God's grace. (Ro 1:8; 2 Thess 1:3)

**My CHARACTER: Justice**
Allow me to know true justice. Guide my responses so that You are pleased by my just behavior. Give me a heart for those who need to receive justice.

**MY COMMITMENT: To Joy**
May all I do be done as unto Christ. Help me to find joy in all tasks that serve others.

**MY FAMILY:** Lord, guide me to be the very best spouse and parent. Help me support and love my family, encouraging them in every way.

**MY LEADERS:** (world, country, local, church, business)
**General:** Lord, I pray that our leaders would be reliable and dependable. (Mt 21: 28-31)
**Pastor:** I ask that the prayer warriors of the congregation be stirred by the Holy Spirit to pray for Pastor _____ . (1 Thess 5:25)

**MY HOPE: David**
I want the **courage** of David, who fought against overwhelming odds in facing the giant Goliath. (1 Sam 17)

> **Question:** Lord, where do I need to show courage in my life today?

> **Question:** Lord, show me if there is someone in my life who needs to be confronted?

Journal your thoughts, make notes, or write your personal prayer:

_____
_____
_____
_____
_____
_____
_____
_____
_____
_____
_____
_____
_____
_____
_____
_____
_____
_____
_____
_____
_____
_____
_____
_____
_____
_____
_____
_____
_____
_____
_____
_____
_____
_____

# Day 27

**MY GOAL:** I want my life to be transformed and compellingly different.

**MY PRAISE:**
MY SHIELD: Father God, I praise You because You are a shield around me. O LORD, You bestow glory on me and lift up my head when I am weary or despised. (Ps 3:3)

**MY THANKS:**
VICTORY: Thanks be to God, who always leads me in triumphal procession in Christ and spreads the knowledge of Him throughout the earth. (2 Cor 2:14)

**MY CHARACTER:**
DISCERNMENT: Father, make me wise enough to recognize when I am not being humble, acceptable, holy, righteous, faithful, just, gentle, meek, forgiving, compassionate, and loving. Fill me with Your power to turn away from sin, and toward You.

**MY COMMITMENT: To Being Christ-like**
I want to be obsessed with imitating You so that I am constantly being shaped into the likeness of Christ.

**MY FAMILY:** Holy Spirit, empower me to do and say the things that will lift up, edify, and encourage my family.

**MY LEADERS:** (world, country, local, church, business)
**General:** Lord, I pray our leaders would be honest in all financial issues and use the Word as a foundation on matters of ethics. (1 Cor 6:10; 1Tim 6:6-10)
**Pastor:** Cause this congregation to respect and honor Pastor
_____. (1 Thessalonians 5:12-13)

**MY HOPE: Elisha**
I want the **boldness** and **trust** of Elisha, who slaughtered his oxen for a BBQ, burned his plow, and followed Elijah. (1 Kings 19:21)

> **Question:** Lord, in what areas do I need to trust you more?

> **Question:** Lord, where do I need a shot of boldness?

Journal your thoughts, make notes, or write your personal prayer:

_____

_____

_____

_____

_____

_____

_____

_____

_____

_____

_____

_____

_____

_____

_____

_____

_____

_____

_____

_____

_____

_____

_____

_____

_____

_____

_____

_____

_____

_____

_____

_____

_____

_____

_____

_____

## Day 28

**MY GOAL:** I want to love God completely – heart, mind, body and soul.

**MY PRAISE:**
GOD OF LIGHT: I praise You, Lord, because You are the light of my salvation. (Ps. 27:1) You know what lies in darkness. Light dwells within You. (Dan 2:22)

**MY THANKS:**
SPIRITUAL SERVICE: I thank Christ, who has given me strength, that He considered me faithful enough to appoint me to His service. (1 Tim 1:12-13)

**MY NEIGHBOR: Do Not Envy One Another**
Lord, help me to be satisfied and keep me from envying others. (Gal 5:26)

**MY COMMITMENT:  To selflessness**
Search my heart, O God, and remove all selfishness and pride. Empower me to think of others first.

**MY FAMILY:**
CONFLICT: Father, I put all existing family conflicts and differences, as well as all potential areas of conflict before Jesus, at the foot of the cross.

**LEADERS:** (world, country, local, church, business)
**General:** Lord, I pray that our leaders seek out, find, and nourish godly friendships. (Ps 1:1-3)
**Pastor:** Father, I ask You to silence any rumors, gossip, or slander that is ever spread about our pastors. (Pr 15:28, 20:19, 21:28)

**MY GOAL: Rahab**
I want the **courage** and **faith** of Rahab, who sheltered the spies. (Joshua 6)

> **Question:** Lord, on what questions do I need the insight of Rahab to determine the right side of an issue?

> **Prayer:** Lord, give me the ability to choose the right course of action.

Journal your thoughts, make notes, or write your personal prayer:

_____
_____
_____
_____
_____
_____
_____
_____
_____
_____
_____
_____
_____
_____
_____
_____
_____
_____
_____
_____
_____
_____
_____
_____
_____
_____
_____
_____
_____
_____
_____
_____
_____
_____

## Day 29

**MY GOAL:** I want to be obsessed with imitating Christ.

**PRAISE:**
COMFORT: Blessed be the Father of our Lord Jesus Christ, the God of mercies and all comfort, who comforts us in all our affliction, so we may comfort those who are in any affliction. (2 Cor 1:3-4)

**MY THANKS:**
JOY: I thank You, Lord, that You, not life's momentary pleasures, are my source of joy. (1 Cor 3:11)

**MY CHARACTER:**
FORGIVENESS: Help me to forgive others as You forgave me. Give me a forgiving attitude, and when possible, the ability to foster reconciliation.

**MY COMMITMENT:**
CONFESSION and REPENTANCE: Lord, give me the courage to openly confess my faults and trespasses. Help me turn away from sin.

**MY FAMILY:**
YOUR WILL: Lord God, change me so that my desires are aligned with Your desires and plans for our family. May Your will be done!

**MY LEADERS:** (world, country, local, church, business)
**General:** Lord, I pray that our leaders would have teachable spirits. (Ro 1:21)
**Pastor:** I pray that our church would be loving, respectful, and understanding of Pastor _____'s family and each other.
(Ephesians 5:25; 1 Peter 3:7; Ephesians 5:33; Ephesians 6:1-4)

**MY HOPE: Daniel**
I want the **faith** and **commitment** of Daniel to **stand firm**. He refused to stop praying to the Lord and was thrown in the den of lions. (Dan 6)

> **Question:** Lord, in what situations do I need the faith of Daniel?

> **Question:** Lord, what areas of rebellion in my life need attention?

Journal your thoughts, make notes, or write your personal prayer:

_____
_____
_____
_____
_____
_____
_____
_____
_____
_____
_____
_____
_____
_____
_____
_____
_____
_____
_____
_____
_____
_____
_____
_____
_____
_____
_____
_____
_____
_____
_____
_____
_____
_____
_____
_____

## Day 30

**MY GOAL:** I want to be an ambassador and servant of the King.

**MY PRAISE:** ANSWER TO PRAYER
I praise and honor You, Father, because You are a God who loves to answer prayer and who begins to answer even before I pray. (Is. 65:24)

**MY THANKS:**
PEACE: Thank you, Lord, for being my source of peace. Please continue to pour out Your peace in my life and let the peace of Christ rule in my heart.

**MY NEIGHBOR: Be Kind to One Another**
Lord, make me a person who never pays back wrong for wrong, but always tries to be kind to everyone. (1 Thess 5:15)

**MY COMMITMENT: To Surrender**
I want to love You completely. Allow my life to show how great You are. Give me strength to step out in faith, even when I don't know the future.

**MY FAMILY:**
HOPE: Lord, give us hope and faith in the Gospel. Help our family to grow and serve while we are being encouraged by the hope of Your Word.

**LEADERS:** (world, country, local, church, business)
**General:** Lord I pray that our leaders would have hearts full of mercy and compassion for the needy, poor, and unfortunate. (Lk 10:33-37)
**Pastor:** Father, I plead that You would strengthen and bless
_____'s marriage and family life. Protect them from the one who would destroy families. (Proverbs 5:15-20)

**MY HOPE: The Other Mary**
I want the **_loyalty and commitment_** to the tenets of our faith like the other Mary and fellow-workers who refused to work on the Sabbath.

> **Question:** Lord, am I doing anything during worship or on Sunday that dishonors You?

> **Prayer:** Lord, help me to be totally dedicated to You.

Journal your thoughts, make notes, or write your personal prayer:

## Day 31

**MY GOAL:** I want to glorify God in everything I do and say.

**MY PRAISE:**
GOD OF ALL: I praise and adore You. As the Holy One of Israel You are my Redeemer; You are the God of all the earth. (Isa 54:5)

**MY THANKS:**
HOPE OF GLORY: I give You thanks that I am justified through faith in my Lord Jesus Christ, through whom I have gained access by faith into His grace. I rejoice in the hope of glory, knowing that You are faithful. (Ro 5:1-5)

**MY NEIGHBOR: Live in Harmony**
Lord, help me to live in harmony with others; to be sympathetic, to love others as brothers, and to be compassionate and humble. (1 Peter 3:8)

**MY COMMITMENT: To Worship**
I want to glorify God every day in all I do and say. Lord God, help me seek after Your heart. Give me the strength to walk in obedience to Your calling in my life and bless me with a life of true worship.

**MY FAMILY:**
SPIRITUAL CONDITION: Father, I pray for a mighty work of Your Holy Spirit to transform the spiritual condition of my immediate and extended family.

**MY LEADERS:** (world, country, local, church, business)
**Pastor:** I pray that _____'s family would be a source of joy and blessing to one another and to the church. (Pr 23:24, 31:28-30)

**MY HOPE: Abraham**
I want the **discernment and blind obedience** of Abraham, who went to an unknown land (Gen 12:1-5), and was willing to sacrifice his only son. (Gen 22)

> **Question:** Lord, in what area am I reluctant to obey Your command?

> **Question:** Lord, is there something I need to do now?

Journal your thoughts, make notes, or write your personal prayer:

_____
_____
_____
_____
_____
_____
_____
_____
_____
_____
_____
_____
_____
_____
_____
_____
_____
_____
_____
_____
_____
_____
_____
_____
_____
_____
_____
_____
_____
_____
_____
_____
_____
_____
_____
_____
_____

"I have made some very unwise
decisions – great mistakes – because
I did not wait patiently upon
the Lord for instruction."

Kay Arthur[5]

# My Life Prayer

**Prayer:** Come, Holy Spirit, fill my heart with Your presence and kindle in me the fire of Your love that I may be renewed and empowered in Your service. Anoint my life with Your power so that I may be the person You have called me to be.

## Introduction

The objective of this section is to briefly list your core values, priorities, goals, and personal characteristics, then use that information to identify your life commitments and formulate a Life Prayer. Most of us have never considered writing down our life goals and commitments. I can tell you personally there is much to be gained from writing them down rather than just thinking, talking, or meditating about them.

You could spend a great deal of time on this subject, but that's not the purpose of this Prayer Guide or this section. The objective here is for you to think seriously about your life, recognize where you are today and record your thoughts. You can spend as much time on this subject as you desire, but my hope is that you spend at least 1-2 hours identifying your values and then however much time it takes you to develop your commitments and write a Life Prayer.

NOTE: If you are not a good writer or don't like to write, just do a list or outline. The journey is far more important than the end result.

## Why bother?

If you don't know where you are going, there is no telling where you will end up! Without purpose and direction it is difficult to make good choices. This examination process produces some very positive results:

- it creates focus and attention,
- it creates action – doing something,
- it begins imprinting on your heart what is truly important,
- it helps reduce distractions and hindrances,
- it creates motivation, and
- it creates desire.

# My Life Values

INSTRUCTION: Read the definitions for each topic below and then on a separate sheet of paper jot down all the answers you can think of without considering whether they are good, bad, right, wrong, etc. Then review the list and choose the top 3-5, and record them here.

## My Character
INSTRUCTION: What is your personal character (good and bad)?

1. _____

2. _____

3. _____

4. _____

5. _____

## My Reputation
INSTRUCTION: What is your reputation today? What do others think of you? How would others describe you?

1. _____

2. _____

3. _____

4. _____

5. _____

## My Strengths

INSTRUCTION: What are your strengths, special skills, and passions?

1. _____

2. _____

3. _____

4. _____

5. _____

## My Weaknesses

INSTRUCTION: What are your weaknesses? What do you dislike?

1. _____

2. _____

3. _____

4. _____

5. _____

## My Life Core Values

DEFINITION: What are the standards by which you live? What values do you cherish? What do you believe in? What values or standards will you absolutely not compromise or violate?

> **LIFE VALUES:** *"The problem with most leaders today is they don't stand for anything. If you don't stand for anything, you'll fall for anything."* (Don Shula)

CORE VALUES: You are likely to have more than 5 core values.

1. _____

2. _____

3. _____

4. _____

5. _____

_____

_____

_____

**My Life Priorities**

DEFINITION: What is most important to you <u>today</u>? What do you value? What do you tend to put first in life? What do your checkbook and calendar indicate are important to you?

1. _____

2. _____

3. _____

4. _____

5. _____


**My Life Goals**

DEFINITION: What do you want to accomplish? What are your dreams? What are your objectives in life? What is your purpose in life?

1. _____

2. _____

3. _____

4. _____

5. _____

## Other

INSTRUCTION: What is important to you that has not been listed above? What important passions are missing? Is there something important in your family, church, career, community, health, education, relationships, finances, spiritual condition, recreation/pleasure, social media, skills and abilities, or character that you have not yet listed?

_____

_____

_____

_____

_____

_____

_____

_____

_____

_____

_____

_____

## My Life Commitments

INSTRUCTION: You can make this topic as brief or extensive as you wish. I suggest a middle-of-the-road approach but you should do what works for you. The initial question is, "What are your personal life commitments?" What commitments do you want to make or what should you make? My own one-page Commitment Statement included subjects like adoration, praise, obedience, service, empowerment, seeking, His will, evangelism (witness), prayer, Bible study, stewardship, being a true disciple, calling, and a final commitment statement.

You might want to review all the work you have done previously in this section and make an initial list of everything you think might be appropriate as a life commitment. Then reduce that list that to something you can work with. I suggest you draft the list on a separate piece of paper and edit before you copy it into your Prayer Guide. Your end product could be a full Commitment Statement, a list of the commitments you want to adopt, or simply the 1-5 commitments that are most important to you.

# SUMMARY
(Review and pray over these subjects periodically.)

**CORE VALUES** (List the 3 most important.)

1. _____

2. _____

3. _____

**LIFE PRIORITIES** (List the 3 most important.)

1. _____

2. _____

3. _____

**LIFE GOALS** (List the 3 most important.)

1. _____

2. _____

3. _____

**COMMITMENTS** (List the 3 commitments that are most important to you.)

1. _____

2. _____

3. _____

## MY LIFE GOAL

INSTRUCTION: Using all the material in this section, finalize a one-sentence statement that represents your spiritual Life Goal. See the first prayer in the 31 Days section for examples.

EXAMPLE: "*I want Jesus to be the central reality of my life.*"

_____

_____

_____

# My Life Prayer

## Example

LORD, fill my heart with Your power, presence, wisdom, and love so I can:

1. discern and walk in Your ways,
2. grow in knowledge and understanding of Your Word,
3. be renewed and empowered in Your service, and
4. glorify You and reveal You to others.

## Your Prayer:

INSTRUCTION: Based on your work in this section, develop a short prayer that summarizes your desire for a right relationship with God. Draft the prayer in such a way that you can memorize it. Make it work for you.

_____

_____

_____

_____

_____

_____

_____

_____

_____

_____

_____

_____

_____

_____

_____

_____

_____

_____

_____

_____

_____

_____

_____

_____

"Upon recognition that prayerlessness was a sin in my life, I was deeply touched by God to make a commitment to pray for one hour a day. Six years (and many "hours") later, God has changed my personality and character, increased my faith through unbelievable answers to prayer, called me to accountability in innumerable areas, and given me a vivid vision of possibilities for His will for my life."

Becky Tirabassi[6]

# Resources

While the prayers and information in the previous sections are intended to be used daily, the following material is primarily for reference purposes. It may be useful when certain issues come to mind or simply be handy for review when needed.

Some of the information will give you a different perspective and food for thought. It is a collection that I have accumulated over the years and have continually gone back and utilized on many occasions. It has also been very helpful to have it close at hand so I am not wasting time searching for it when I need it.

This material warrants more than casual reading. I would encourage you to review this section and become familiar with the topics covered.

The contents of this section are not intended to be exhaustive but rather provide you an adequate foundation for further use. This material is generally not covered in other parts of the Prayer Guide.

# 1. Apostles' Creed

I believe in God, the Father Almighty,
creator of heaven and earth.
I believe in Jesus Christ, his only Son, our Lord.

He was conceived by the power of the Holy Spirit
and born of the Virgin Mary.
He suffered under Pontius Pilate,
was crucified, died, and was buried.
He descended to the dead.
On the third day he rose again.
He ascended into heaven,
and is seated at the right hand of the Father.
He will come again to judge the living and the dead.

I believe in the Holy Spirit,
the holy catholic* Church,
the communion of the saints,
the forgiveness of sins,
the resurrection of the body,
and the life everlasting.

Amen.

*Note: when the word "catholic" is used here, it means "the universal church" and not the Roman Catholic Church.

## 2. Armor of God

Stand your ground, putting on the belt of truth and the body armor of God's righteousness. For shoes, put on the peace that comes from the Good News so that you will be fully prepared. In addition to all of these, hold up the shield of faith to stop the fiery arrows of the devil. Put on salvation as your helmet, and take the sword of the Spirit, which is the word of God. Pray in the Spirit at all times and on every occasion. Stay alert and be persistent in your prayers for all believers everywhere. (Ephesians 6:14-18 NLT)

### Prayer

**Belt of Truth:** The Word of God is Truth. The enemy is the father of lies. I know that _____ is not from God, and I reject it in Jesus' name. (2 Tim 1:7)

**Breastplate of Righteousness:** I am in Christ! He has paid my sin debt and set me free. I am a sinner saved by Grace. I claim the righteousness of Christ. (2 Cor 5:21)

**Shoes of the Gospel of Peace:** I commit to having Gospel conversations. Jesus Christ died and rose again as full atonement for my sins, and I stand on His shed blood as the foundation of my salvation. I will proclaim the Gospel to all who will listen.

**Shield of Faith:** The Bible says that no weapon formed against me will prevail. (Isa 54:17; Eph 6:16) If wounded by an arrow that penetrates my shield of faith, I claim my status as a child of the Living God.

**Helmet of Salvation:** I have been delivered from eternal hell and given the gift of salvation through Christ. I stand on the Word of God and the shed blood of my Savior and His resurrection. (Romans 6:6-11)

**Word of the Spirit:** I believe the Word of God and pray it over my circumstances, good and bad. I claim His perfect love over me, and claim His Word as protection against the enemies of God.

**Praying in the Spirit for Saints:** I pray the Armor of God over _____. I ask that they be protected from the lies of the enemy.

## 3. Beatitudes (Mt 5:3-10 NIV)

Blessed are the *poor in spirit,*
>            for theirs is the kingdom of heaven.

Blessed are those who *mourn,*
>            for they will be comforted.

Blessed are the *meek*,
>            for they will inherit the earth.

Blessed are those who hunger and *thirst for righteousness*,
>            for they will be filled.

Blessed are the *merciful*,
>            for they will be shown mercy.

Blessed are the *pure in heart*,
>            for they will see God.

Blessed are the *peacemakers,*
>            for they will be called sons of God.

Blessed are those who are *persecuted* because of righteousness,
>            for theirs is the kingdom of heaven.


What is my lifestyle if I live according to these Beatitudes? What do I have or do?

| | |
|---|---|
| poor in spirit | **spiritual poverty or bankruptcy; I am humble** |
| mourn | **deep sadness over sin; I realize how God <u>hates</u> sin** |
| meek (gentle) | **humility before God; I "walk humbly with my God" (Micah 6:8)** |
| righteous | **zeal for righteousness; I am honest; I live with integrity** |
| merciful | **bring relief to the miserable; I actively do something** |
| pure in heart | **committed to pure lifestyle; I act rightly even when it's difficult** |
| peacemakers | **bring reconciliation; I put myself in the middle and risk some flak** |
| persecuted | **stand firm; I will not be moved; I am fully committed** |

# 4. Who is a Truly Committed Christ-follower?

1. **Intentional Obedience**: I will intentionally commit my life to be obedient to Your Word.

2. **Intimate Worship**: I will earnestly seek to worship in spirit and truth; I will celebrate the majesty of Your Name!

3. **Spiritual Growth**: I will zealously meditate on and study the Word of God.

4. **Fervent Prayer**: I will diligently pray for personal transformation, for the Church, for the hurting, and for the lost.

5. **Humble Service**: I will humbly serve God by actively serving people in true loving kindness. I will faithfully use my gifts, talents, and skills in ministry, serving God and His Church.

6. **Thankful Giving**: I will tithe to the church and share with those in need.

7. **Intentional Faith-based Conversations:** I will actively pursue conversations about God's truth with others.

8. **Committed Relationships**: I will encourage and be accountable to other Christ-followers.

9. **Faithful Attendance**: I will faithfully and regularly attend my local church. I will be an active participant, offering my gifts and skill in service.

10. **Divine Power**: I will passionately seek His presence and power in my life in order to accomplish all of the above.

NOTE:
These commitments were produced by a group of 10-12 local church leaders who met for two hours each week, prayed, discussed, and arrived at these ten answers to the question: *Who is a truly committed Christ-follower?* I was privileged to lead this group.

## 5. Christian Living

This list combines all the commands in the following passages and provides a summary outline in three categories.
(Col 3:1-17, 4:2-6; Eph 4 and 5; Ro 12:4-13:14;  and 1 Thes 4 and 5:12-22)

### Christ-like Character:

**Love:**          Love one another and others as yourself.
**Forgive:**       Forgive one another.
**Peace:**         Live at peace with everyone.
**Truth:**         Speak truthfully in love; do not lie.
**Patience:**      Be patient in your afflictions and trials.
**Humility**:      Be humble; honor others above yourself.
**Joyful:**        Be joyful.
**Righteous**:     Be compassionate, kind, gentle, good,
                   wise, hospitable, and decent; do what is right.

### Avoid Sin:

**Change**:        Take off the old self, and put on the new creation in Christ.
**Anger**:         Get rid of bitterness, rage, and anger.
**Sex**:           Avoid sexual immorality, impurity, and lust.
**Evil**:          Avoid evil and overcome evil with good.
**Drunkenness:**   Do not get drunk.
**Work**:          Do not steal, but work. Be useful; don't be idle.
**Speech**:        Avoid unwholesome talk; put off obscenity, foolish
                   talk, coarse joking, slander, and filthy language.

### Act and Serve:

**Opportunity:**   Make the most of every opportunity.
**Knowledge:**     Know what you are talking about.
**Thanks:**        Give thanks to God for everything.
**Singing**:       Speak to others and God with psalms, hymns, and songs.
**Prayer:**        Be faithful and devoted in prayer.
**The Needy:**     Share with those in need.
**Enemies:**       Bless your enemies and those who persecute you.
**Debt:**          Repay everyone what you owe them.
**Strangers:**     Be wise in the way you treat outsiders.
**Unity:**         Build up the church to reach unity in the faith.
**Leaders:**       Respect your pastors and hold them in high regard;
                   be on guard against false teachers.

## 6. Creation Scriptures

The fool says in his heart, "*There is no God*." (Ps 14:1)

Neh 9:6    Father, Creator, Maker of Heaven and earth, I praise You because You alone are the LORD. You made the heavens, even the highest heavens, and all their starry host, the earth and all that is on it, the seas and all that is in them. You give life to everything, and the multitudes of heaven worship you. (NIV)

Gen 1:1    In the beginning God created the heavens and the earth. (NIV)

Jer 10:12    But God made the earth by his power; he founded the world by his wisdom and stretched out the heavens by his understanding. (NIV)

Isaiah 6:3    Holy, holy, holy is the LORD Almighty; the whole earth is full of his glory. (NIV)

Isaiah 40:12    Who has measured the waters in the hollow of his hand, or with the breadth of his hand marked off the heavens? Who has held the dust of the earth in a basket, or weighed the mountains on the scales and the hills in a balance? (NIV)

Psalms 8:3-4    When I consider your heavens, the work of your fingers, the moon and the stars, which you have set in place, what is man that you are mindful of him, the son of man that you care for him? (NIV)

Psalms 19:1-4    The heavens declare the glory of God; the skies proclaim the work of his hands. Day after day they pour forth speech; night after night they display knowledge. There is no speech or language where their voice is not heard. Their voice goes out into all the earth, their words to the ends of the world. In the heavens he has pitched a tent for the sun. (NIV)

Psalms 147:4-5    He determines the number of the stars and calls them each by name. Great is our Lord and mighty in power; his understanding has no limit. (NIV)

Psalms 47:7    For God is the King of all the earth; sing to him a psalm of praise. (NIV)

## 7. Daniel's Prayer for the City
[Source: Daniel 9:4-19 (NIV modified by SHB)]

O Lord, the great and awesome God, who keeps His covenant of love with all who love Him and obey His commands, we have sinned and done wrong. We have been wicked and have rebelled; we have turned away from Your commands and laws. We have not listened to our pastors and religious leaders, who spoke in Your name to our secular leaders, our families and to all the people of the land.

7 Lord, You are righteous, but this day we are covered with shame – the men and women of our city and country – Your people. We have been unfaithful. O LORD, we and our secular leaders are covered with shame because we have sinned against You. The Lord our God is merciful and forgiving. However, we have rebelled against You; we have not obeyed or kept the laws You gave us through Your Word. All the people of our country have transgressed Your laws and turned away, refusing to obey You. Therefore the curses and judgments written in Your Word have been poured out on us, because we have sinned against You. You have fulfilled the words spoken against us and against our leaders by bringing judgment upon us. Just as it is written in Your Word, this judgment has come upon us, yet we have not sought Your favor by turning from our sins and giving attention to Your truth. You did not hesitate to bring judgment upon us, for the LORD our God is righteous in everything He does; yet we have not obeyed.

15 Now, O Lord our God, who sent Your Son to deliver His people, and who made for Yourself a name that endures to this day, we have sinned, we have done wrong. O Lord, in keeping with all Your righteous acts, turn away Your anger and Your wrath from our city. Our sins of our fathers have made our city and Your church an object of scorn to all those around us.

17 Now, our God, hear the prayers and petitions of Your people. For Your sake, O Lord, look with favor on Your desolate church. Give ear, O God, and hear; open Your eyes and see the desolation of our cities. We do not make requests of You because we are righteous, but because of Your great mercy. O Lord, listen! O Lord, forgive! O Lord, hear and act! For Your sake, O my God, do not delay, because our cities and Your people bear Your Name.

## 8. Family Prayer Time

### 1. Encourage your family to pray.
Help your family become aware of answered prayer. Tell them about the times in your life when God answered your prayers.

### 2. Help your family appreciate God's creation and blessings.
Thank Him publically. Mention it during grace before meals.

### 3. Have a family prayer and devotion time.
Pray for the special needs and concerns of your children or grandchildren.

### 4. Pray for people in need.
Pray with your family about issues and problems you're aware of. It might be something on the news or simply for a friend's situation.

### 5. Adopt special people to pray for.
Pray for the needs of a people group, missionary, unsaved person, city, church, government leader, etc.

### 6. Pray for family traditions, trips, and events.
Lay hands on and pray for your children or grandchildren on their birthdays.

### 7. Maintain a family prayer log.
Record the needs and the answers to your prayers.

### 8. Prayer walk in your neighborhood with your family.
Pray for the neighbors around you, both those you know and those you don't know. Prayer walk around your school, church, or workplace.

## 9. Fasting

### Definition
Fasting is giving up something significant for a predetermined period of time. Fasting should be directed at either (1) elevating the presence of God in your life (coming closer to God), or (2) a very specific spiritual purpose (maybe some sin in your life). It is the voluntary denial of something that will cause you to focus on a spiritual problem or goal.

### What to fast from
The item given up is often food but it could be TV, alcohol, smoking, reading, sexual relations, sports, social media, electronics (TV, smartphones, computers, radio), news feeds, politics, fitness, or anything that tends to be important in your life.

### Why is fasting important?
Fasting brings urgency, priority, resolution, tenacity, gravity, importance, and seriousness to our praying. It gives it a force and power. Fasting is a powerful weapon against spiritual apathy.

God asks us to humble ourselves (Mt 18:4; 23:12; James 4:10 and 1 Peter 5:6). Fasting is one effective way to walk humbly with our God. It is not the only way, but one that is clearly outlined in Scripture. (Lev 16:29-31; Ps 35:13; Ezk 8:21) God clearly required fasting under Old Testament doctrine. But what does the New Testament say about fasting?

### Jesus fasted
Jesus fasted before His confrontation with Satan.

### New Testament
The New Testament church is under no Scriptural doctrine to fast, except as led by the Spirit. Personal and corporate fasting are certainly appropriate, particularly if called by church leaders, but long, permanent, or rigid fasting is not consistent with Scripture.

### Private not public
Fasting should normally be done privately. Friends and outsiders have no need to know you are fasting. It is between you and God.

## The benefits of fasting

1. It helps you draw closer to God.

2. It improves your prayer life.

3. It reminds you that God created and sustains us.

4. It helps us focus on what is important. What are the real priorities of life?

5. It brings clarity in decision making.

6. It increases our patience, perseverance, and discipline.

## Guidelines for fasting from food

1. Don't fast if you are sick or have health issues. Check with your doctor.

2. Don't fast if you need an immediate answer to a question or concern. Fasting is not likely to produce answers to time-critical questions.

3. Be led by God into fasting. Be sure your motives are right.

4. Always drink adequate amounts of water.

5. Start slowly. Don't begin with a 7-day fast. Start with one meal or one day. Extend your fasts as you desire once you are comfortable with the process. Educate yourself on fasting before you begin.

6. If you decide to fast regularly, make sure you have adequate recovery time. Your body will need to time adjust to a new routine.

7. An ideal way to begin a 24-hour fast is to begin after your evening meal. Thus, you will only miss breakfast and lunch.

8. Recover slowly. Don't eat a big meal after a fast. The longer the fasting period, the more slowly you should ease back to your normal routine.

## 10. God's Names

God revealed His Names to us so that we might know Him and His true character. Each name reveals a different aspect of His character.

**Three Major Names:**

| 1. | God | *Elohim* | powerful |
| 2. | LORD | *I AM (Yahweh)* | covenant God ("Jehovah") |
| 3. | Lord | *Adonai* | master |

**Other Names:**

| 4. | | *El Elyon* | most high |
| 5. | | *El Shaddai* | almighty |
| 6. | | *Jehovah Jireh* | provides |
| 7. | | *Jehovah Rophe* | heals |
| 8. | | *Jehovah Nissi* | my banner |
| 9. | | *Jehovah Mekadesh* | sanctifies |
| 10. | | *Jehovah Shalom* | peace |
| 11. | | *Jehovah Tsidkenu* | righteousness |
| 12. | | *Jehovah Rohi* | shepherd |

**He Proclaimed His Name, the LORD (Yahweh):**

Exodus 34:5-7    Then the LORD came down in the cloud and stood there with him and proclaimed his name, the LORD. And he passed in front of Moses, proclaiming, "The LORD, the LORD, the compassionate and gracious God, slow to anger, abounding in love and faithfulness, maintaining love to thousands, and forgiving wickedness, rebellion and sin. Yet he does not leave the guilty unpunished; he punishes the children and their children for the sin of the fathers to the third and fourth generation." (NIV)

**The Psalms tell us how to use His Name:**

- Ps 99:6    The godly **pray** to Him by calling on His Name.
- Ps 20:7    The godly **trust** in His Name.
- Ps 52:9    The godly **hope** in His Name.
- Ps 7:17    The godly **sing praise** to His Name.
- Ps 89:16    The godly **rejoice** in His Name.
- Ps 69:36    The godly direct **love** to His Name.
- Ps 61:5    The godly direct **fear** to His Name.

## 11. Healing Prayer

Lord, as _____'s Creator, I pray that You would grant healing to
_____. Let Your healing presence surround _____ and bring
the healing that is needed.

Lord, Your name declares that You are the Healer. Be true to Your Name and
bring healing into _____'s life.

I praise You, O God, because You heal and make things whole. I pray in the
name of Jesus that You would heal and make _____ whole.

Father, I pray that You will heal _____ because of Jesus' sacrifice
on the cross. Because of His shed blood, I pray that You would give healing
to _____.

Lord, I pray that _____ would reach out to You and receive
Your healing power when _____ reaches out.

Lord Jesus, You are Lord over all, including sickness and disease. In the Your
mercy and divine power, I pray that You would remove/heal _____
in _____'s life.

Father, thank you for Your mercy and compassion. _____ is
suffering and needs Your healing touch. I implore you to release Your
healing power in _____'s life.

Father, in the name of Jesus I pray for You to heal _____
so that You might receive glory, honor, and praise. Grant healing to
_____ so that the watching world would recognize
and worship You because of Your love, compassion, and power.

Father, I know You have the power to heal and I believe that You are willing
to heal. I bring _____ to Your altar of grace and pray
that You would provide complete healing. In faith, I claim Your healing
power in _____ life.

## 12. Idols

| Money | Self | Approval | Control |
|---|---|---|---|
| Pleasure | Food | Sleep | Darkness |
| Cursing | Abundance | The World | Possessions |

**Love of money:** I pray that I would not love money or have a sinful longing for it. Do not allow my pursuit of money to be more important to me than my pursuit of knowing, loving, and obeying You. (1 Timothy 6:10)

**Love of self:** I ask that I would not love myself more than You. Deliver me from being self-centered and grant me the power and strength to deny myself. (2 Timothy 3:2)

**Love of approval:** Father, I pray that I will love and seek Your approval above the approval of men. Cause me to pursue a lifestyle of pleasing You rather than men. (John 12:42)

**Love of control:** Father, enable me to overcome the desire for power. I ask that You create in me a servant's heart and willingness to serve others. (3 John 9:10)

**Love of pleasure:** I beg that I will not love pleasure more than You. Cause me to find my greatest delight and pleasure in You. (2 Tim 3:4)

**Love of food:** I want You, not food, to be my God. Cause me to have the proper perspective when it comes to food. (Prov 21:17)

**Love of sleep:** Enable me to get the proper rest, but deliver me from indulging in too much sleep and laziness. (Proverbs 20:13)

**Love of darkness:** I pray that I would not love my sin more than You. Cause me to hate sin and love You with all my being. (Jn 3:19)

**Love of cursing:** I pray that I would not choose speaking profanity and filth over speaking words of love and encouragement. (Ps 109:17)

**Love of abundance:** I ask that gaining material possessions would not be the pursuit of my life. I ask that You would grant me the grace and power to love You and pursue You above all else. (Eccl 5:10)

**Love of the things of the world:** Lord, do not allow me to love the attitudes or values of this world more than I love You. Deliver me from the lust of the flesh and eyes and the pride of life. I want to love You more than this world. (1 Jn 2:15)

## 13. Jesus' Prayer – John 17

Most scholars outline this chapter based on the three different groups of people Jesus prayed for:

| | |
|---|---|
| 17:1-5 | Himself |
| 17:6-19 | existing disciples |
| 17:20-23 | future disciples (the church) |

We can list what Jesus prayed for each group:

Himself:

| | |
|---|---|
| 17:1 | to be glorified |
| 17:2-4 | His mission |
| 17:5 | reinstatement of previous glorified state |

Existing Disciples:

| | |
|---|---|
| 17:6-10 | their status and situation |
| 17:11-16 | that they would be preserved and protected |
| 17:17-19 | that they would be sanctified |

Future Disciples:

| | |
|---|---|
| 17:21-22 | unity |
| 17:20-23 | that the world would know God sent Jesus |

Five themes can be easily identified:

### A. Giving:

The theme of what God gives Jesus or believers and what Jesus gives His followers is spread throughout the chapter:

| | |
|---|---|
| 17:2 | eternal life |
| 17:4 | work |
| 17:8, 14 | His words |
| 17:11-12 | name |
| 17:13 | His joy |
| 17:5, 22, 24 | His glory |
| 17:26 | love |

### B. Unity:

The three kinds of unity are described in the prayer:

| | |
|---|---|
| 17:1-6, 7, 21 | Christ in unity with the Father |
| 17:10, 21, 23 | Believers in unity with Christ and God |
| 17:11, 21, 23 | Believers in unity with other believers |

### C. Glory:

The word "glory" occurs seven times with various meanings in the chapter. The primary implication is that Jesus will reveal the source of that glory. What does Ps 86:9-12 tell us about glorifying God?

(a) to praise His name, and

(b) to honor His commandments

### D. Disciple:

In verses 17:6-8, Jesus outlines what it means to be a disciple:

| | |
|---|---|
| 17:6 | to understand we were chosen by God |
| 17:6 | to obey God's commands and decrees |
| 17:7-8 | to believe and know Jesus came from God |
| 17:10 | to bring glory to Jesus |

### E. World:

Jesus gave His disciples instructions regarding the world in John 17:14-23:

- They should live in the world, not withdraw from it.
- They should demonstrate their faith to the world.
- They should face the troubles of the world.
- They should make it known that Jesus was sent by God.

Jesus knew that remaining in the world would be challenging and dangerous for the disciples. They would need the power of His name for protection. Hostility toward Jesus and God would fall on the heads of the disciples. But Jesus called down the power of God's name so that they could be one in will and purpose.

**Praying John 17**

### John 17:1-5

I pray that I will know, exalt, and honor Christ so that He is glorified through me by the successful completion of the work He gives me to do.

### John 17:6-19

I pray that I will believe, accept, and obey the Word of Truth so that I might:
- reveal it to my friends and others that I meet;
- be protected from the evil one by the power of His Name;
- be one with Christ as He is one with God the Father;
- have the joy of Christ in me; and
- be truly sanctified.

### John 17:20-26

I pray that I will be one with other believers and one with Christ in order that I might proclaim the Gospel and the love of God through word and deed, all to the glory of God.

## 14. Jesus' Prayers

**Matt 11:25-26**    At that time Jesus said, "I praise you, Father, Lord of heaven and earth, because you have hidden these things from the wise and learned, and revealed them to little children. Yes, Father, for this was your good pleasure." (NIV)

**Matt 14:23**    After he had dismissed them, he went up on a mountainside by himself to pray. When evening came, he was there alone. (NIV)

**Matt 15:36**    Then he took the seven loaves and the fish, and when he had given thanks, he broke them and gave them to the disciples, and they in turn to the people. (NIV)

**Matt 19:13**    Then little children were brought to Jesus for him to place his hands on them and pray for them. But the disciples rebuked those who brought them. (NIV)

**Matt 26:26-27**    While they were eating, Jesus took bread, gave thanks and broke it, and gave it to his disciples, saying, "Take and eat; this is my body." Then he took the cup, gave thanks and offered it to them, saying, "Drink from it, all of you." (NIV)

**Matt 26:36**    Then Jesus went with his disciples to a place called Gethsemane, and he said to them, "Sit here while I go over there and pray." (NIV)

**Matt 26:39**    Going a little farther, he fell with his face to the ground and prayed, "My Father, if it is possible, may this cup be taken from me. Yet not as I will, but as you will." (NIV)

**Matt 26:42**    He went away a second time and prayed, "My Father, if it is not possible for this cup to be taken away unless I drink it, may your will be done." (NIV)

**Matt 26:44**    So he left them and went away once more and prayed the third time, saying the same thing. (NIV)

Matt 27:46　About the ninth hour Jesus cried out in a loud voice, *"Eloi, Eloi, lama sabachthani*?" – which means, "My God, my God, why have you forsaken me?" (NIV)

Mark 1:35　Very early in the morning, while it was still dark, Jesus got up, left the house and went off to a solitary place, where he prayed. (NIV)

Mark 6:41　Taking the five loaves and the two fish and looking up to heaven, he gave thanks and broke the loaves. Then he gave them to his disciples to set before the people. He also divided the two fish among them all. (NIV)

Mark 6:46　After leaving them, he went up on a mountainside to pray. (NIV)

Mark 14:32-39　They went to a place called Gethsemane, and Jesus said to his disciples, "Sit here while I pray." He took Peter, James and John along with him, and he began to be deeply distressed and troubled. "My soul is overwhelmed with sorrow to the point of death," he said to them. "Stay here and keep watch." Going a little farther, he fell to the ground and prayed that if possible the hour might pass from him. "Abba, Father," he said, "everything is possible for you. Take this cup from me. Yet not what I will, but what you will." Then he returned to his disciples and found them sleeping. "Simon," he said to Peter, "Are you asleep? Could you not keep watch for one hour? Watch and pray so that you will not fall into temptation. The spirit is willing, but the body is weak." Once more he went away and prayed the same thing. (NIV)

Luke 3:21　When all the people were being baptized, Jesus was baptized too. And as he was praying, heaven was opened. (NIV)

Luke 5:16　But Jesus often withdrew to lonely places and prayed. (NIV)

Luke 6:12　One of those days Jesus went out to a mountainside to pray, and spent the night praying to God. (NIV)

Luke 9:18　Once when Jesus was praying in private and his disciples were with him, he asked them, "Who do the crowds say I am?" (NIV)

Luke 9:28-29    About eight days after Jesus said this, he took Peter, John and James with him and went up onto a mountain to pray. As he was praying, the appearance of his face changed, and his clothes became as bright as a flash of lightning. (NIV)

Luke 11:1    One day Jesus was praying in a certain place. When he finished, one of his disciples said to him, "Lord, teach us to pray, just as John taught his disciples." (NIV)

Luke 22:32    "But I have prayed for you, Simon, that your faith may not fail. And when you have turned back, strengthen your brothers." (NIV)

Luke 22:41-44    He withdrew about a stone's throw beyond them, knelt down and prayed, "Father, if you are willing, take this cup from me; yet not my will, but yours be done." An angel from heaven appeared to him and strengthened him. And being in anguish, he prayed more earnestly, and his sweat was like drops of blood falling to the ground. (NIV)

Luke 23:34    Jesus said, "Father, forgive them, for they do not know what they are doing." And they divided up his clothes by casting lots. (NIV)

John 11:41-42    So they took away the stone. Then Jesus looked up and said, "Father, I thank you that you have heard me. I knew that you always hear me, but I said this for the benefit of the people standing here, that they may believe that you sent me." (NIV)

John 12:27-28    "Now my heart is troubled, and what shall I say? `Father, save me from this hour'? No, it was for this very reason I came to this hour. Father, glorify your name!" Then a voice came from heaven, "I have glorified it, and will glorify it again." (NIV)

1 Cor 11:24    . . . and when he had given thanks, he broke it and said, "This is my body, which is for you; do this in remembrance of me." (NIV)

Heb 5:7    During the days of Jesus' life on earth, he offered up prayers and petitions with loud cries and tears to the one who could save him from death, and he was heard because of his reverent submission. (NIV)

## 15. Knowing God

I want to know God in order to:

**Avoid Punishment:** He will punish those who do not know God and do not obey the gospel of our Lord Jesus. (2 Thes 1:8 NIV)

**Gain Freedom:** Formerly, when you did not know God, you were slaves to those who by nature are not gods. But now that you know God – or rather are known by God – how is it that you are turning back to those weak and miserable principles? (Gal 4:9 NIV)

**Love:** Dear friends, let us love one another, for love comes from God. Everyone who loves has been born of God and knows God. Whoever does not love does not know God, because God is love. (1 John 4:7-8 NIV)

**Attain the Resurrection:** I want to know Christ and the power of his resurrection and the fellowship of sharing in his sufferings, becoming like him in his death, and so, somehow, to attain to the resurrection from the dead. (Phil 3:10-1 NIV)

**Prayer:**
Father, I need to acquaint myself with the mighty, sovereign, holy, and majestic God who is the Creator of heaven and earth. I desire the peace and rest that comes from knowing You. Give me an urgent desire to seek and know Your ways.

Your Word says that we will come to know You if we are obedient to Your commands. Lord, give me the ability to walk in Your ways. Make Your presence known to me because of my obedience. Lord, I want You to be the priority in my life. Empower me to seek knowledge of You in all things. Bless me with understanding and knowledge of Your ways. Amen

## 16. Listening

Some answers to prayer require hearing or listening to God. If you are seeking direction, guidance, or advice you need to hear God's answer. That hearing may come from a leading of the Holy Spirit, or it may come from reading God's Word, or it may come as advice from a Christian friend – all of which require listening.

Many of the New Testament words used for "listening" imply the concept of active hearing or listening, and sometimes understanding or obeying. The key to active listening is doing it with intention. You must want to hear what God or the Bible or another person is saying. You must give them and their words the respect they deserve by listening attentively. Scripture offers some helpful insight on this skill:

- Be swift to hear, slow to speak. (James 1:19)
- Listening requires study. (Proverbs 15:28)
- Withholding unnecessary words shows wisdom. (Proverbs 17:27, 28)
- Fools reveal their lack of understanding by their words. (Proverbs 18:2)

In the Gospels, Luke 8:18 says, "Therefore, consider carefully how you listen. Whoever has will be given more; whoever does not have, even what he thinks he has will be taken from him." (NIV) Clearly, active listening is important and there are rewards for those who earnestly listen.

### Wait for silence

Place yourself in His presence and become quiet. As you wait, block out background noise, deepen your sense of God, and quiet your heart.

Ps 46:10    Be still, and know that I am God; I will be exalted among the nations, I will be exalted in the earth. (NIV)

Ps 27:14    Wait for the Lord; be strong and take heart and wait for the Lord. (NIV)

## Listen for instruction

Intentionally visualize yourself in the presence of Jesus, and listen.

> 1 Sam 3:9    So he said to Samuel, "Go and lie down again, and if someone calls again, say, 'Speak, Lord, your servant is listening.'" So Samuel went back to bed. (NLT)

## Be confident and expectant

> 1 John 5:14    This is the confidence we have in approaching God: that if we ask anything according to his will, he hears us. (NIV)

> Eph 3:12    In him and through faith in him we may approach God with freedom and confidence. (NIV)

## Conclusion

Listening is more than just hearing. It is hearing and understanding. It is connecting with what the other person is saying. A close personal relationship requires communication and listening on both sides. I know God hears me – I also know that I don't always hear God because I don't take the time to stop and listen. How about you?

## Prayer

Lord, be constantly before me. May Your Word abide in me so that I can pray in Your will. Give me the patience to listen. Help me (enable me) to wait and watch expectantly throughout the day for Your activity.

## 17. Lord's Pryer

**Our Father, in Heaven.**
Recognizing God as "Father" implies that we are His children, part of the family of God. He is the creator and sustainer of life and He cares about us as would a parent or shepherd.

**Hallowed be Your name.**
"Hallowed" means holy. We must acknowledge and give honor and praise to God. God's honor should be a top priority, and our lives should honor and proclaim His Name.

**Your kingdom come, Your will be done.**
We acknowledge God as ruler of the world. He is our King and Sovereign Lord. We must choose to obey His will. Our lives should reflect His plan. He should be the priority in our lives and His commandments should rule our lifestyle.

**Give us each day our daily bread.**
TODAY: Our God is in control. He is sovereign and will provide for all our needs. God provides and I accept what He gives, regardless of the size or type of His daily provision. I put my future and well-being in His hands.

**Forgive our sins, as we forgive those who sin against us.**
YESTERDAY: We examine our relationships and repair those that need to be fixed. Jesus forgives us so we understand the desire to forgive others. But our forgiveness for sin comes only from the grace of God and the shed blood of Christ. We do not take revenge or hold grudges against others.

**And lead us not into temptation, but deliver us from evil.**
TOMORROW: We pray to God for His protection and deliverance. He will walk through every valley with us and hold our hand when necessary. Our struggle is with the dark powers of evil and spiritual forces in the heavenly realms. We need the power of God to protect us from Satan. Thus, we put on the full armor of God.

**For Yours is the kingdom, power, and glory forever. Amen!**
The prayer ends with praise and a focus on God, and the word "Amen," which means "So be it."

# 18. Meditation Topics

**My Prayer**
Am I persevering in prayer to the extent necessary to release God's power?

**My Commitment**
Does my commitment and action unlock patience and perseverance?

**My Vision**
We live our lives because of a vision, not for temporal events.

**My Desires**
What are the true inner desires of my heart?

**My Discipline**
Discipline and intentionality produce spiritual reflexes of the heart.

**My Life**
What does it look like if Jesus is the central reality in my life?
What is God currently doing in my life?
What is God saying to me today?
How am I doing in my walk with the Lord?
What do I need to discover about myself that only God knows?
What are my true life priorities?
How could my speech be a source of healing?
How is my thought life?

**My Jesus**
What does it mean to "keep my eyes on Jesus"?
How could I imitate Jesus?
How would I describe Jesus?

**My Core Values**
What are my core values?
How has the world corroded my core values?

**My Hope**
Who or what is my hope?

## 19. Nicene Creed

We believe in one God, the Father, the Almighty
maker of heaven and earth, and of all that is, seen and unseen.

We believe in one Lord, Jesus Christ,
   the only Son of God,
   eternally begotten of the Father,
   God from God, Light from Light,
   true God from true God,
   begotten, not made, one in Being with the Father.
   Through him all things were made.
   For us men and for our salvation,
   he came down from heaven:
   by the power of the Holy Spirit
   he was born of the Virgin Mary, and became man.
   For our sake he was crucified under Pontius Pilate;
   he suffered, died, and was buried.
   On the third day he rose again
   in fulfillment of the Scriptures;
   he ascended into heaven
   and is seated at the right hand of the Father.
   He will come again in glory to judge
   the living and the dead,
   and his kingdom will have no end.

We believe in the Holy Spirit,
   the Lord, the giver of life,
   who proceeds from the Father and the Son.
   With the Father and the Son he
   is worshipped and glorified.
   He has spoken through the Prophets.
   We believe in one holy catholic*
   and apostolic Church.
   We acknowledge one baptism
   for the forgiveness of sins.
   We look for the resurrection of the dead,
   and the life of the world to come. Amen.

*See page 118.

## 20. One Another Verses (ESV)

### Love

John 13:34-35   A new commandment I give to you, that you love one another: just as I have loved you, you also are to love one another. By this all people will know that you are my disciples, if you have love for one another. [Also: Gal 5:14; 1 John 3:11, 23; 1 John 4:7, 11-12; 1 John 4:21; 2 John 5; Rom 13:8, 10; James 2:8; Matt 5:43-44; Matt 19:19; Mark 12:31; 1 Peter 1:22]

### Encourage and build up

1 Thess 5:11   Therefore encourage one another and build one another up, just as you are doing. [Also: Ro 14:19; Heb 10:24-25; Ro 15:2]

### Exhort

Heb 3:13-14   But exhort one another every day, as long as it is called "today," that none of you may be hardened by the deceitfulness of sin.

### Stir up to good deeds

Heb 10:24   And let us consider how to stir up one another to love and good works.

### Kind

Eph 4:32   Be kind to one another, tenderhearted, forgiving one another, as God in Christ forgave you. [Also: 1 thess 5:15]

### Harmony

Rom 12:16   Live in harmony with one another. Do not be haughty, but associate with the lowly. Never be conceited. [Also 1 Peter 3:8]

### Accept

Rom 15:7   Therefore welcome one another as Christ has welcomed you, for the glory of God.

### Serve

Gal 5:13   For you were called to freedom, brothers. Only do not use your freedom as an opportunity for the flesh, but through love serve one another.

## Resources

### Share burdens

Gal 6:2    Bear one another's burdens, and so fulfill the law of Christ.
[Also: Eph 4:2; Col 3:13]

### Teach and admonish

Col 3:16    Let the word of Christ dwell in you richly, teaching and admonishing one another in all wisdom, singing psalms and hymns and spiritual songs, with thankfulness in your hearts to God.

### Pray

James 5:16    Therefore . . . pray for one another, that you may be healed. The prayer of a righteous person has great power as it is working.

### Confess

James 5:16a    Therefore, confess your sins to one another.

### Judgment

Rom 14:13a    Therefore let us not pass judgment on one another any longer. [Lk 6:37a; Ro 2:1-3; James 4:11-12]

### Slander

James 4:11a    Do not speak evil [slander] against one another, brothers.
[Also: Lev 19:16; Pr 11:12-13]

### Provoke

Gal 5:26    Let us not become conceited, provoking one another.

### Envy

Gal 5:26    Let us not . . . envy one another.

### Truth

Eph 4:25    Therefore, having put away falsehood, let each one of you speak the truth with his neighbor, for we are members one of another.

### Stumbling block

Rom 14:13    Therefore let us not pass judgment on one another any longer, but rather decide never to put a stumbling block or hindrance in the way of a brother. [Also: 1 Cor 8:11-13]

### Wash feet

John 13:14    If I then, your Lord and Teacher, have washed your feet, you also ought to wash one another's feet.

### Forgive

Eph 4:32b    . . . forgiving one another, as God in Christ forgave you.
[Mt 6:14-15; Col 3:13b; Matt 18:21-22, 35; Luke 17:3-4]

**Golden rule:** (Do unto others as you would have them do unto you.)
Luke 6:31    And as you wish that others would do to you, do so to them.
[Also: Mt 7:12]

### Submit

Eph 5:21    . . . submitting to one another out of reverence for Christ.

### Boast

2 Cor 10:17-18    Let the one who boasts, boast in the Lord. For it is not the one who commends himself who is approved, but the one whom the Lord commends.

### Humility

1 Peter 5:5    Likewise, you who are younger, be subject to the elders. Clothe yourselves, all of you, with humility toward one another, for "God opposes the proud but gives grace to the humble."
[Also: 1 Pet 3:8; Pr 27:2; Phil 2:3]

### Interests

Phil 2:4    Let each of you look not only to his own interests, but also to the interests of others.

### Teach

Col 3:16a    Let the word of Christ dwell in you richly, teaching and admonishing one another in all wisdom. [Also: 2 Tim 2:2; Ro 15:14]

### Hospitable

1 Peter 4:9    Show hospitality to one another without grumbling.
[Also: Rom 16:16a]

**Resources**

### Unity
Eph 4:2-3   . . . bear with one another in love, eager to maintain the unity of the Spirit in the bond of peace. [Also: 1 Cor 1:10; 1 Cor 12:25]

### Compassion
Zech 7:9   Thus says the Lord of hosts . . . show kindness and mercy to one another. [Also: 1 Peter 3:8]

### Fellowship
1 John 1:7   But if we walk in the light, as he is in the light, we have fellowship with one another, and the blood of Jesus his Son cleanses us from all sin.

### Reconciliation
Matt 5:24   . . . leave your gift there before the altar and go. First be reconciled to your brother, and then come and offer your gift.

### Care
1 John 3:17-18   But if anyone has the world's goods and sees his brother in need, yet closes his heart against him, how does God's love abide in him? Little children, let us not love in word or talk but in deed and in truth. [Also: James 2:15-16; Pr 3:29-30; Pr 14:21]

### Hate
1 John 4:20   If anyone says, "I love God," and hates his brother, he is a liar; for he who does not love his brother whom he has seen cannot love God whom he has not seen. [Also 1 John 2:9-11]

## 21. Paul's Prayers (NIV)

### Eph 1:15-23
For this reason, ever since I heard about your faith in the Lord Jesus and your love for all the saints, I have not stopped giving thanks for you, remembering you in my prayers. I keep asking that the God of our Lord Jesus Christ, the glorious Father, may give you the Spirit of wisdom and revelation, so that you may know him better. I pray also that the eyes of your heart may be enlightened in order that you may know the hope to which he has called you, the riches of his glorious inheritance in the saints, and his incomparably great power for us who believe. That power is like the working of his mighty strength, which he exerted in Christ when he raised him from the dead and seated him at his right hand in the heavenly realms, far above all rule and authority, power and dominion, and every title that can be given, not only in the present age but also in the one to come. And God placed all things under his feet and appointed him to be head over everything for the church, which is his body, the fullness of him who fills everything in every way.

### Eph 3:16-21
I pray that out of his glorious riches he may strengthen you with power through his Spirit in your inner being, so that Christ may dwell in your hearts through faith. And I pray that you, being rooted and established in love, may have power, together with all the saints, to grasp how wide and long and high and deep is the love of Christ, and to know this love that surpasses knowledge – that you may be filled to the measure of all the fullness of God. Now to him who is able to do immeasurably more than all we ask or imagine, according to his power that is at work within us, to him be glory in the church and in Christ Jesus throughout all generations, for ever and ever! Amen.

### Eph 6:18-20
Pray in the Spirit on all occasions with all kinds of prayers and requests. With this in mind, be alert and always keep on praying for all the saints. Pray also for me, that whenever I open my mouth, words may be given me so that I will fearlessly make known the mystery of the gospel, for which I am an ambassador in chains. Pray that I may declare it fearlessly, as I should.

### Phil 1:3-6
I thank my God every time I remember you. In all my prayers for all of you, I always pray with joy because of your partnership in the gospel from the first day until now, being confident of this, that he who began a good work in you will carry it on to completion until the day of Christ Jesus.

## Resources

### Phil 1:9-11
And this is my prayer: that your love may abound more and more in knowledge and depth of insight, so that you may be able to discern what is best and may be pure and blameless until the day of Christ, filled with the fruit of righteousness that comes through Jesus Christ – to the glory and praise of God.

### 1 Thes 1:2-3
We always thank God for all of you, mentioning you in our prayers. We continually remember before our God and Father your work produced by faith, your labor prompted by love, and your endurance inspired by hope in our Lord Jesus Christ.

### 1 Tim 2:1-2
I urge, then, first of all, that requests, prayers, intercession and thanksgiving be made for everyone – for kings and all those in authority, that we may live peaceful and quiet lives in all godliness and holiness.

### 2 Tim 1:3-4
I thank God, whom I serve, as my forefathers did, with a clear conscience, as night and day I constantly remember you in my prayers. Recalling your tears, I long to see you, so that I may be filled with joy.

### 1 Cor 1:4-9
I always thank God for you because of his grace given you in Christ Jesus. For in him you have been enriched in every way – in all your speaking and in all your knowledge – because our testimony about Christ was confirmed in you. Therefore you do not lack any spiritual gift as you eagerly wait for our Lord Jesus Christ to be revealed. He will keep you strong to the end, so that you will be blameless on the day of our Lord Jesus Christ. God, who has called you into fellowship with his Son Jesus Christ our Lord, is faithful.

### 2 Cor 13:7, 9
Now we pray to God that you will not do anything wrong. Not that people will see that we have stood the test but that you will do what is right even though we may seem to have failed. We are glad whenever we are weak but you are strong; and our prayer is for your perfection.

### Col 1:3-6
We always thank God, the Father of our Lord Jesus Christ, when we pray for you, because we have heard of your faith in Christ Jesus and of the love you have for all the saints – the faith and love that spring from the hope that is stored up for you in heaven and that you have already heard about in the word of truth, the gospel that has come to you.

## Col 1:9-14

For this reason, since the day we heard about you, we have not stopped praying for you and asking God to fill you with the knowledge of his will through all spiritual wisdom and understanding. And we pray this in order that you may live a life worthy of the Lord and may please him in every way: bearing fruit in every good work, growing in the knowledge of God, being strengthened with all power according to his glorious might so that you may have great endurance and patience, and joyfully giving thanks to the Father, who has qualified you to share in the inheritance of the saints in the kingdom of light. For he has rescued us from the dominion of darkness and brought us into the kingdom of the Son he loves, in whom we have redemption, the forgiveness of sins.

## Col 2:1-3

I want you to know how much I am struggling for you and for those at Laodicea, and for all who have not met me personally. My purpose is that they may be encouraged in heart and united in love, so that they may have the full riches of complete understanding, in order that they may know the mystery of God, namely, Christ, in whom are hidden all the treasures of wisdom and knowledge.

## Col 4:2-6, 12

Devote yourselves to prayer, being watchful and thankful. And pray for us, too, that God may open a door for our message, so that we may proclaim the mystery of Christ, for which I am in chains. Pray that I may proclaim it clearly, as I should. Be wise in the way you act toward outsiders; make the most of every opportunity. Let your conversation be always full of grace, seasoned with salt, so that you may know how to answer everyone. Epaphras, who is one of you and a servant of Christ Jesus, sends greetings. He is always wrestling in prayer for you, that you may stand firm in all the will of God, mature and fully assured.

## 1 Thes 3:10-13

Night and day we pray most earnestly that we may see you again and supply what is lacking in your faith. Now may our God and Father himself and our Lord Jesus clear the way for us to come to you. May the Lord make your love increase and overflow for each other and for everyone else, just as ours does for you. May he strengthen your hearts so that you will be blameless and holy in the presence of our God and Father when our Lord Jesus comes with all his holy ones.

## 1 Thes 5:16-18

Be joyful always; pray continually; give thanks in all circumstances, for this is God's will for you in Christ Jesus.

## Resources

### 2 Thes 1:11-12
With this in mind, we constantly pray for you, that our God may count you worthy of his calling, and that by his power he may fulfill every good purpose of yours and every act prompted by your faith. We pray this so that the name of our Lord Jesus may be glorified in you, and you in him, according to the grace of our God and the Lord Jesus Christ.

### 2 Th 3:1-2
Finally, brothers, pray for us that the message of the Lord may spread rapidly and be honored, just as it was with you. And pray that we may be delivered from wicked and evil men, for not everyone has faith.

## Notes on the prayers of Paul:

_____

_____

_____

_____

_____

_____

_____

_____

_____

_____

_____

_____

_____

_____

_____

_____

_____

_____

_____

_____

_____

_____

_____

_____

# 22. Personal Awakening – How to pray

Lord, I pray for:

- GOD: a deep awareness of God,

- SIN: an intense sensitivity toward sin,

- WORD: a continuing desire for understanding God's Word,

- PRAYER: a gripping concentration for prayer,

- HOLINESS: personal purity and a desire for holiness,

- CHURCH: a strengthened commitment to Your church,

- HARMONY: harmony in my family and in the church,

- WITNESS: an enthusiasm for gospel conversations, and

- JUSTICE: an increased desire for social justice.

## 23. Personal Prayer Retreat

### Why a retreat?

We need special times:

- of intense communication with God,
- of personal reflection and meditation,
- to seek His direction and will for our lives,
- for difficult situations for ourselves and others, and
- to recharge and energize our power source.

### The details:

WHEN: What time will you begin? I suggest an early start: sunrise is a great time to begin! Set a length of time and hold to it.

WHERE: Where will you go? Find a place with few distractions.

WHAT: What is the agenda? Prayer and meditation are obvious. Reading the Bible or other inspirational reading can also be useful.

WHO: Your retreat can be personal or shared with a prayer partner or small group.

RESOURCES: Take with you writing materials, Bible, this Prayer Guide, and necessary electronics for research.

FOOD/DRINK: Taking your own food means you won't interrupt the flow of your experience by going to a restaurant.

GOALS: Make note of particular goals you have for your retreat. What do you want to accomplish? Write them down in advance.

### Agenda:

- Plan your retreat carefully.
- Build it around a specific need or concern.
- Plan for some time on your knees if you are physically able.
- Alternate physical activity: sit, stand, walk, and kneel.
- Plan time for listening.
- Build in time for writing or journaling.

## Come Holy Spirit:

As you prepare and participate in the prayer retreat, ask the Holy Spirit to guide you. The Holy Spirit can assist your prayers, influence your meditations, and be your companion throughout the day. But you must ask.

## Possible Subjects

1. The Sermon on the Mount (Mt 5-7)

2. The Beatitudes (Mt 5:1-12)

3. The Armor of God (Eph 6)

4. The Lord's Prayer (Mt 6:9-15)

5. Your Life Prayer (Prayer Guide, p 115)

6. Prayer of St. Francis (Prayer Guide, p 162)

7. The Apostle's Creed (Prayer Guide, p 118)

8. The Attributes of God

9. The Promises of God

## Guidelines

1. **Preparation**: Plan what you are going to do. One week in advance begin praying for your retreat.

2. **Listen**: Be prepared to listen!

3. **Persevere**: Don't give up if it feels unproductive. Have an agenda for the day and a timeframe for different activities. Spend some time walking and praying in order to bring variety to your day.

4. **Sin**: If you have a habitual sin, deal with it first so that it does not block the progress of your day.

5. **Journal**: Take notes on any important thoughts or guidance you receive.

6. **Worship**: End your retreat with thanksgiving and praise.

## 24. Power Prayer

[Based on "Daily Disciplines for the Christian Man," Dr. Bob Beltz, NavPress, ISBN 978-0891097655.]

**STEP 1: I admit my need.**
Father, I am spiritually powerless, and apart from Your divine intervention in my life, I do not have the ability to surrender to Your ways.

**STEP 2: I confirm God's power.**
Father, You are almighty. Empower me to be a true disciple. Intervene in my life so I can be all You want me to be.

**STEP 3: I hold on to the vine.**
Holy Spirit, fill my life today with Your presence, power, and grace. Live the life of Christ in and through me today. Help me hold on to the Vine.

**STEP 4: I surrender to the Lordship of Christ.**
Jesus, I give up the throne of my life. I put my crowns at Your feet and I beg You to take control as Lord of my life.

**STEP 5: I seek forgiveness and cleansing.**
Lord Jesus, I am a sinner in need of Your grace. Forgive my sinful nature and the sinful actions that dishonor You. I confess, repent, and will make restitution where appropriate.

**STEP 6: I want a real relationship with Christ.**
Through prayer, Bible study, and fellowship I am determined to improve my relationship with Jesus. I will seek to know and do the will of God through the power of the Holy Spirit

**STEP 7: I will serve in the Kingdom.**
Lord Jesus, by Your grace and with Your help I will seek to make You the central reality of my life. I will serve You in my home, my community, my workplace, and my church. Live Your life through me today.

# 25. Prayer Walking

[Source: "*Prompts for Prayer Walkers: Seven Ways to Pray from God's Word for Your World*," Steve Hawthorne, WayMakers, www.waymakers.org]

## General

Prayer walking is praying kingdom-sized prayers for specific places, locations, homes, buildings, schools, neighborhoods, etc. Our physical presence at a specific location helps us relate to the subject – our prayers become more real. Prayer walking is praying specifically for situations where the subject intersects with our own needs and interests. For example, parents or grandparents might prayer walk around a school building.

## Low-profile

"Prayer walking is usually a low-profile affair: Friends or family stroll two-by-two through their own neighborhoods, schools, and work places, praying as they go. Once in a while the prayers can be demonstrative, but usually it's fairly quiet. It's being on the scene without making one. Though they usually walk unnoticed, prayer walkers quickly become aware of the realities and needs of their neighbors."

## The process

1. Form a team
You can do it alone but it's more effective to pray with others. Groups of two or three seem to work best.

2. Identify a location
Know where you are going and the route you will follow. A short route usually is best. Alternatively you could pray from a high point in the area.

3. Choose a topic
Know what you are praying for or about. You might choose a related verse from scripture.

4. Finish with a discussion
Discuss your walk with your partners. What did you learn in observing the location? What should you pray about next time?

# 26. Praying For Israel and Jerusalem

Source: http://www.prayingscriptures.com

## Historical perspective

Those who have cursed God's people have paid dearly over the centuries. Israel and Jerusalem are dear to the heart of God. The Bible states that the nations will be judged according to their position on Israel. (Joel 3) Israel as a nation and a people are God's chosen people. In Deut 32:10 and Zechariah 2:8, the Lord God calls Israel "the apple of His eye." God said in Genesis 12:2-3 that He would bless those who blessed Israel, and whoever curses Israel He would curse.

Paul wrote in Romans 10:1 that the longing of his heart and his prayer to God was that Israel would be saved. The Bible tells us how to pray:

## Rescue from trouble

Ps 25:22    O God, ransom Israel from all its troubles. (NLT)

## Know God

Isa 45:3    And I will give you treasures hidden in the darkness — secret riches. I will do this so you may know that I am the Lord, the God of Israel, the one who calls you by name. (NLT)

## Eternal salvation

Isa 45:17    But the Lord will save the people of Israel with eternal salvation. Throughout everlasting ages, they will never again be humiliated and disgraced. (NLT)

## Healing, prosperity, and peace

Jer 33:6    Nevertheless, the time will come when I will heal Jerusalem's wounds and give it prosperity and true peace. (NLT)

## Forgiveness

Jer 33:8    I will cleanse them of their sins against me and forgive all their sins of rebellion. (NLT)

## Refuge
Joel 3:16    The Lord's voice will roar from Zion and thunder from Jerusalem, and the heavens and the earth will shake. But the Lord will be a refuge for his people, a strong fortress for the people of Israel. (NLT)

## Provide needs
Joel 2:19    The Lord will reply, "Look! I am sending you grain and new wine and olive oil, enough to satisfy your needs. You will no longer be an object of mockery among the surrounding nations." (NLT)

## Peace
Pr 16:7    When people's lives please the Lord, even their enemies are at peace with them. (NLT)

## Shepherd
Ezek 34:12-14    I will be like a shepherd looking for his scattered flock. I will find my sheep and rescue them from all the places where they were scattered on that dark and cloudy day. (NLT)

## Spiritual wisdom and insight
Eph 1:17-18    . . . asking God, the glorious Father of our Lord Jesus Christ, to give you spiritual wisdom and insight so that you might grow in your knowledge of God. I pray that your hearts will be flooded with light so that you can understand the confident hope he has given to those he called — his holy people who are his rich and glorious inheritance. (NLT)

## 27. Promises About Prayer in the Bible (NLT)

### He will respond

HE ANSWERS: I am praying to You because I know You will answer, O God. Bend down and listen as I pray. (Ps 17:6)

HE ANSWERS: [God says,] I will answer them before they even call to me. While they are still talking about their needs, I will go ahead and answer their prayers! (Isa 65:24)

HE RESCUES: When they call on me, I will answer; I will be with them in trouble. I will rescue and honor them. (Ps 91:15)

HE RESPONDS: O people of Zion, who live in Jerusalem, you will weep no more. He will be gracious if you ask for help. He will surely respond to the sound of your cries. (Isa 30:19)

HE GIVES: If you need wisdom, ask our generous God, and he will give it to you. He will not rebuke you for asking. (James 1:5-6)

### He hears

MY VOICE: Morning, noon, and night I cry out in my distress, and the Lord hears my voice. (Ps 55:17)

PRAYERS OF THE RIGHTEOUS: The Lord is far from the wicked, but he hears the prayers of the righteous. (Pr 15:29)

### He commands us to pray

COME BOLDLY: So let us come boldly to the throne of our gracious God. There we will receive his mercy, and we will find grace to help us when we need it most. (Heb 4:16)

## He tells us how to pray

IN SECRET: But when you pray, go away by yourself, shut the door behind you, and pray to your Father in private. Then your Father, who sees everything, will reward you. (Mt 6:6)

IN THE SPIRIT: Pray in the Spirit at all times and on every occasion. Stay alert and be persistent in your prayers for all believers everywhere. (Eph 6:18)

FOR YOUR ENEMIES: But I say, love your enemies! Pray for those who persecute you! (Mt 5:44-45)

## He gives us conditions for answered prayer

This subject is covered in the Introduction. References are to Matthew 7:7-8, Matthew 21:22, John 14:14, John 15:7-8, and 1 John 3:22.

## Miscellaneous

WISDOM: Ask me and I will tell you remarkable secrets you do not know about things to come. (Jer 33:3-4)

HOLY SPIRIT: And the Holy Spirit helps us in our weakness. For example, we don't know what God wants us to pray for. But the Holy Spirit prays for us with groanings that cannot be expressed in words. (Romans 8:26-27)

CONFESSION: Confess your sins to each other and pray for each other so that you may be healed. The earnest prayer of a righteous person has great power and produces wonderful results. (James 5:16-17)

## 28. Quotes From E. M. Bounds

*Purpose in Prayer*, E. M. Bounds, Baker Book House, Grand Rapids MI, (New Edition), Copyright 1991 by Baker Book House Company, ISBN: 0-8010-1010-1

"It is only when the whole heart is gripped with the passion of prayer that the life-giving fire descends." (p 19)

"Everything depends on prayer, and yet we neglect it not only to our own spiritual hurt but also to the delay and injury of our Lord's cause upon the earth." (p 25)

"I think Christians fail so often to get answers to their prayers because they do not wait long enough on God." (p 31)

"We must not only pray, but we must also pray with great urgency, with intentness, and with repetition." (p 43)

"Too often we get faint-hearted and quit praying at the point where we ought to begin. We let go at the very point where we should hold on the strongest. Our prayers are weak because they are not impassioned by an unfailing and irresistible will." (p 48)

"The men who have done mighty things for God have always been mighty in prayer, have well understood the possibilities of prayer, and made most of these possibilities." (p 73)

"When prayer fails, the world prevails, when prayer fails the church loses its divine characteristics, its divine power; the church is swallowed up by a proud ecclesiasticism, and the world scoffs at its obvious impotence." (p 74)

"If we are abiding in Christ . . . then there lie open before us the infinite resources of the divine treasure-house." (p 87)

NOTE:
For nearly 100 years E. M. Bounds' books on prayer have stimulated and inspired the church to pray. He was a man of God who lived to pray. Edward McKendree Bounds (1835-1913) began each day with three hours of prayer.

# 29. Revival: Praying for the Church

1. LOVE: Father, cause Your people to love You and each other each other with all their heart, soul, mind, and strength. (Matthew 22:39)

2. PRAISE: Father, I pray You will create a spirit of praise in the church. (Ps 150)

3. PRAYER and FASTING: Father, create a desire for prayer and fasting in our church. (Colossians 4:2)

4. SINFUL NATURE: O Lord, heal our backsliding and sinful actions. Turn Your anger away from us. (Hosea 14:4)

5: VISION: Lord, give us a powerful vision of Your holiness. (Isaiah 6)

6. PRESENCE: Lord, do not take away our ability to sense Your presence. Help us to abide in Your presence. (Psalm 51:11)

7. REPENT: Father, cause the believers in our church to repent of anything in our lives that would hinder our experience of revival. (Luke 3:4-6) Grant a spirit of brokenness and repentance in our church. (Isaiah 57:15) Cause the people to acknowledge their sin. (Psalm 51:3)

8. FOCUS ON SELF: Lord Jesus, break the believers of our church from a spirit of self-sufficiency. Grant us a spirit of trust and dependence on You. (Rev 2:17)

9. RESTORATION: Though our sins testify against us, restore the believers of this church for Your great name's sake. (Jeremiah 14:7)

10. TRUE SALVATION: Father, I pray that You will convict and save those who belong to this church but who have been deceived about true salvation and are not saved. Have mercy on them and save them. (Matthew 23:27-28)

## 30. Saint Francis' Prayer

Lord, make me an instrument of Your peace.
      where there is hatred, let me sow love;
      where there is injury, pardon;
      where there is doubt, faith;
      where there is despair, hope;
      where there is darkness, light;
      where there is sadness, joy.

O Divine Master, grant that I may not so much seek
      to be consoled as to console;
      to be understood as to understand;
      to be loved as to love.

For it is in giving that we receive;
it is in pardoning that we are pardoned; and
it is in dying that we are born to eternal life.

Amen

# 31. Prayer for Unity

I pray for:

1.  INTERCESSORS: that many men and women will be raised up to pray for unity in the church.

2.  ONE ACCORD: that the church will be of one accord and that differences on non-doctrinal issues will be put aside in order to proclaim and serve the Lord.

3.  SERVICE: that believers in different congregations will come together in unity to serve the real needs of our local community.

4.  WITNESS: that the love and unity between different churches will be obvious to the non-believing public. I pray that believers of all churches in the community will demonstrate humility, gentleness, patience, love, and peace toward one another.

5.  HUMILITY: that the purpose of coming together will be to help those served and not to elevate ourselves. I pray that walls that have been built between different congregations and denominations will come crashing down as we serve each other with a humble spirit.

6.  CLARITY: that the result of unity will be a new effectiveness, strength, and clarity in proclaiming the Gospel message.

7.  LEADERS: that pastors and lay leaders will be raised up to equip the church, and they will have patience and perseverance in serving the church in unity.

8.  SPIRITUAL GROWTH: that in working together our own faith will be encouraged and the church will grow spiritually.

## 32. Worship That is Acceptable

*"Where people are not stunned by the greatness of God, how can they be sent with the ringing message, 'Great is the Lord and greatly to be praised; he is to be feared above all Gods!'" (Ps 96:4) Savoring the vision of a triumphant God in worship precedes spreading it to others. All of history is moving toward one great goal, the worship of God among the peoples of the earth. The great sin of the world is that we have failed to delight in God so to reflect His glory. For God is most reflected in us when we are most delighted in Him."*

*John Piper*

**Definition:** Worship is the ceremony or response we offer to express our devotion, allegiance, and honor to God. It can be the direct acknowledgement of His presence, nature, ways, or claims. Worship can be either inward acts (love, joy, trust, adoration, etc.) or outward expressions (service, prayer, posture, praise, singing, dancing, giving, etc.).

### 1. We must worship rightly (acceptably).
Heb 12:28-29    Therefore . . . let us be thankful, and so worship God acceptably with reverence and awe. (NIV)

### 2. We can approach God directly.
1 Peter 2:9    But you are a chosen people, a royal priesthood, a holy nation, a people belonging to God, that you may declare the praises of him who called you out of darkness into his wonderful light. (NIV)

### 3. We must worship God through Christ.
John 10:9    I am the gate; whoever enters through me will be saved.
John 14:6    I am the way and the truth and the life. No one comes to the Father except through me. (NIV)

### 4. God is holy; I must be free of sin.
Heb 10:4, 10    [It] is impossible for the blood of bulls and goats to take away sins . . . 10 And by that will, we have been made holy through the sacrifice of the body of Jesus Christ once for all. (NIV)
Psalms 24:3-4    Who may ascend the hill of the LORD? Who may stand in his holy place? He who has clean hands and a pure heart, who does not lift up his soul to an idol or swear by what is false. (NIV)

### 5. My life is an act of worship.

Romans 12:1    Therefore, I urge you, brothers, in view of God's mercy, to offer your bodies as living sacrifices, holy and pleasing to God – this is your spiritual act of worship. (NIV)

### 6. We must bring the message of light and life.

Matt 5:16    . . . let your light shine before men, that they may see your good deeds and praise your Father in heaven. (NIV)

### 7. Our worship must be rooted in the Word.

John 6:35    Then Jesus declared, "I am the bread of life. He who comes to me will never go hungry, and he who believes in me will never be thirsty." (NIV)

### 8. Our worship is a matter of the heart.

Mark 12:30    Love the Lord your God with all your heart and with all your soul and with all your mind and with all your strength. (NIV)

It is important to focus on what the Old Testament tabernacle foreshadowed: Christ. It is also critical to understand that our worship can be unacceptable to God when it is:

| | | |
|---|---|---|
| • | Ignorant – we know not what we do | (Jn 4:22) |
| • | Improper – idolatrous | (Ro 1:22-23) |
| • | Inferior – God wants only our best | (Mal 1:8) |
| • | In vain – following the rules of men | (Mt 15:9) |

How does authentic worship occur? John Piper says that the joy that results in magnifying God must come from a true understanding of His glory. If our worship is unsatisfying, it may be because there is a lack of the Word of God. Religious feelings or responses that do not come from a true understanding of God are not holy, no matter how intense. We can wave our hands all we want, but if we do not know God or understand His ways, what are we doing? Feigned activity is unacceptable.

True worship must include inward feelings that reflect our gratitude and joy for the love and grace of God. Hypocritical worship is going through the motions (singing, dancing, jumping, etc.) which outwardly indicate affections that do not really exist.

"Faith comes from looking at God,
not at the mountain."

Bill Hybels[7]

# Introduction to the Prayer of Jabez

The following Bible study comes from The OBSCURE Bible Study Series. This lesson was published in Book 4 of the series titled, *God at the Center* *(https://www.amazon.com/dp/B08T7TL1B1)*. The Series is published with a separate Leader Guide that contains answers to the discussion questions. I have included here the Personal Study Guide but provided the discussion answers at the end of the study.

Because the lessons in this study were developed for both individual study and small group discussions the answers tend to be extensive in order to make it easy to lead a group discussion.

## Why a Bible Study in a Prayer Guide?

The answer is because the story of Jabez and his prayer are unique in the Bible. There are only two verses that mention Jabez and his prayer, but they have an important message and lesson to teach us:

- It is acceptable to pray for blessings for yourself.
- It hints strongly as to why God answered this prayer.
- It suggests our motives and how we could pray.
- It makes us consider if our prayers are big enough.

## Recommendation

Invite a few friends to study this prayer together. You have the publisher's permission to photocopy the Jabez prayer study which follows and give it to your friends for the purpose of having a small group study.

# *Jabez*

he prayed for blessing

**Occurrences of "Jabez" in the Bible: 3**

**Themes: Prayer**

## Scripture

1 Chronicles 4:9-10    ESV
*Jabez was more honorable than his brothers; and his mother called his name Jabez, saying, "Because I bore him in pain." 10 Jabez called upon the God of Israel, saying, "Oh that you would bless me and enlarge my border, and that your hand might be with me, and that you would keep me from harm so that it might not bring me pain!" And God granted what he asked.*

1 Chronicles 4:9-10    HCSB
*Jabez was more honorable than his brothers. His mother named him Jabez and said, "I gave birth to him in pain." 10 Jabez called out to the God of Israel: "If only You would bless me, extend my border, let Your hand be with me, and keep me from harm, so that I will not cause any pain." And God granted his request.*

1 Chronicles 4:9-10    NKJV
*Now Jabez was more honorable than his brothers, and his mother called his name Jabez, saying, "Because I bore him in pain." 10 And Jabez called on the God of Israel saying, "Oh, that You would bless me indeed, and enlarge my territory, that Your hand would be with me, and that You would keep me from evil, that I may not cause pain!" So God granted him what he requested.*

> NOTE: Some translations translate, "*so that it might not bring me pain*"(ESV) as a request not to cause pain to someone else. Both interpretations are reasonable given the original text, but they provide different perspectives. The HCSB and NKJV above provide this latter interpretation in comparison with the ESV.

## The Context

This passage occurs in the middle of a series of genealogies describing the ancestry of the Hebrew nation. Chapters 1 and 2 trace the Israelites history from Adam through Caleb's sons. Chapter 3 describes David's descendants, and Chapter 4 lists other descendants of Judah. It's here that we find Jabez. In general, no information is given other than the names linked to the parents. However, occasionally a little more detail is provided, and this is how we learn more about Jabez. This is the only place in the Bible Jabez or his prayer is mentioned.

## What Do We Know?

The passage says that Jabez was more honorable than his brothers, but it does not explain what that means. It also tells us that he was birthed in pain but there is no explanation of that statement either.

We are told of a prayer Jabez prayed:

- He asked to be blessed.
- He asked that his border [or *territory*] be enlarged meaning an increase of his wealth and influence.
- He asked that God's hand to be upon him, that is, God's protection and empowerment.
- He asked that he would be protected from harm and pain, or that he would not cause pain.

Lastly, and perhaps most importantly, we are told that God granted his requests. These are very straightforward requests. One might think that asking for blessing is presumptuous, but apparently God found it acceptable as the text tells us He granted the request. Jabez's first request, "bless me," is very general. It is reasonable to look at the remainder of the requests as specific ways in which he wishes to be blessed.

## Implications and Observations

First and foremost in making any observations about this prayer and its implications, we should remember that God answered the prayer. Therefore, we must assume that the prayer was acceptable and appropriate.

**Jabez**

Given the fact that God granted Jabez's requests, what might we assume about those requests? First, blessings are available and God will grant them. Second, wealth and power are not inherently bad, and God is willing to grant them to those He chooses. Third, He will empower us in some or in many areas of our lives, but we may need to ask. Fourth, pain and evil are real and we need protection from it.

Finally, we need to pray with the right motives. Jabez did not wish to be harmed or cause harm that might result in pain in his life or the life of another. Having the right motive is also confirmed in the New Testament:

> James 4:3    *You ask and do not receive, because you ask wrongly, to spend it on your passions.* ESV

We have two hints in this passage as to why God might have chosen to answer this prayer:

- Jabez was more honorable than his brothers, and
- He asked God to prevent him from causing pain (HCSB and NKJV).

If the HCSB and NKJV translations are closer to the correct understanding, we observe a humble spirit in Jabez in his desire not to cause pain to others. Obviously God knows Jabez's heart and in the end, that may determine whether God is going to answer a prayer of this magnitude.

## Discussion Questions

A. GENERAL

A1.  Why would the author include this extra information about Jabez? What makes his prayer worthy of mention?

A2.  What do you think it means that Jebez was "more honorable than his brothers"?

A3.  List other prayers the Bible tells us God answered.

A4.  After God answered this prayer, what other requests might Jabez need or want to pray? For each of his requests, how might Jabez expand his prayer to ensure a desired result?

- Be blessed.

- Increase territory.

- Protection and empowerment

- Protected from harm or evil.

- Not cause pain.

A5.  How can we pray this prayer and not be selfish? What is our <u>motive</u>?

## B.  BORDER (Territory)

B1.  Territory (land) was a fundamental wealth component during the time of Jabez. If you were praying a similar prayer today, what might you pray for? Why?

**Jabez**

B2. What other areas of life (other than wealth or influence) could you ask to be expanded?

Q. In which one of these areas could you personally have the biggest impact? Why?

B3. Is it appropriate to pray for wealth?

B4. If "territory" represents relationships, in what ways do you think God might want you to enlarge your personal territory? Why?

## C. BLESSING

C1. Jabez's first request was to be blessed. Do you think it is appropriate to ask God to bless you?

C2. When you ask for blessing what are you personally thinking you are asking for? What are you expecting?

C3. How do you think God responds to an "open-ended" honest request for blessing? (An open-ended request means there are no specifics.)

C4. What would your life look like if God poured out His blessing on you and your family? In what areas of your life would He be most likely to bless you? Why?

C5. Do you think God's blessings are conditional or unconditional? Why? Why not?

## D. POWER

D1. Was there a time in your life when you asked for God's power?
What happened?

D2. What are some of the excuses we all give for staying in our comfort zones?

**Jabez**

## E.  EVIL

E1.  What evil do you want God to protect you from?  Are there areas of your life that you play close to the edge where you would desire God's power to keep you safe?

E2.  If Satan designed a trap or temptation to snare you, what would it be? Or what is your greatest weakness? We are normally vulnerable at our weak points.

## F.  APPLICATION

F1.  What, if anything, are you doing today that requires God's power, other than life in general?

F2.  Do you have not because you ask not? Does your prayer life need to improve and become more focused?

F3.  Are you asking for the things you need or for what you want?

F4.  Do your prayers have eternal significance? For example, do you pray:

> That my life would bring praise and honor to God.
>
> That I would know God.
>
> That I have a right relationship with Christ.
>
> That my worship is acceptable and heartfelt.
>
> That I thirst for the truth of God's Word.
>
> That I love God with all my heart, strength, mind, soul.
>
> That Christ is the central focus and reality of my life.
>
> That I always have a thankful heart.

F5.  Are your prayers big enough?

## Challenge Exercise:

Expand each section of Jabez's prayer. Rewrite the prayer so that it is personal, in modern terms, and adds substance to your request. I have expanded the first request. Do at least one of the others for yourself.

"Bless Me"

*Lord, I desire Your blessing! Please pour out in my life every possible blessing You desire for me. Father, I want You working in my life and I need the guidance and direction of the Holy Spirit so that my walk is pleasing to You. Bless me so that I can be a blessing to others. I desire Your blessing so that You receive honor and thanksgiving from others who see You working in my life. Bless me O Lord.  AMEN.*

> Q.  When you read the above what strikes you?  What do you notice about this prayer?

**Jabez**

<u>Expanded Prayer</u>

Subject: _____

Prayer: _____

_____

_____

_____

_____

_____

_____

_____

_____

_____

_____

_____

_____

_____

_____

# ANSWERS to Jabez Discussion Questions

## A. GENERAL

A1. Why would the author include this extra information about Jabez? What makes his prayer worthy of mention?
*He models the type of prayer God might answer.
*Like the Lord's Prayer, we have a template or example of how to pray.
*We can consider the two reasons that God might have answered the prayer:
 *Jabez asked for God to prevent him from causing pain (HCSB), and
 *Jabez was more _honorable_ than his brothers.

A2. What do you think it means that Jebez was "more honorable than his brothers"?
*He deserved respect.
*He demonstrated honest or moral behavior.
*He was fair or proper.
*He was decent.
*He was ethical, honest, or just.
*He was noble, respected, or upstanding.

A3. List other prayers the Bible tells us God answered.
*Elijah (1 Kings 17-18): drought, then rain.
*Daniel (6:16): lion's den.
*Daniel (3:18): fiery furnace.
*Moses praying over the battle: Ex 17:10ff.

A4. After God answered this prayer, what other requests might Jabez need or want to pray? For each of his requests, how might Jabez expand his prayer to ensure a desired result?
**Be blessed.**
 *Respond appropriately to blessing.
 *Respond with thanksgiving.
**Increase territory.**
 *Not love money, wealth, or power.
 *Have wisdom to manage the expanded "territory."
**Protection and empowerment**
 *Sense God's direction.
 *Ability to obey.
**Protected from harm or evil.**
 *Protect from temptation.
 *Resist the devil and flee evil.
**Not cause pain.**
 *Guard the tongue!
 *Consider how actions impact others.

A5. How can we pray this prayer and not be selfish? What is our _motive_?
*Use answers to this prayer to do good (Eph 2:10).
*Point people to Christ.

**Jabez**

*Glorify God.
*Cause people to give thanks to God.
*Serve others.
*Develop Fruit of the Spirit.

## B. BORDER (Territory)
B1.  Territory (land) was a fundamental wealth component during the time of Jabez. If you were praying a similar prayer today, what might you pray for? Why?
*Use of wealth. Pray for the strength and wisdom to use any expanded or additional wealth wisely, whatever the type or amount.

B2.  What other areas of life (other than wealth or influence) could you ask to be expanded?
*Relationships.
*Ministry or service.
*Political success.
*Character (attributes).
*Job or career.

   Q.  In which one of these areas could you personally have the biggest impact? Why?

B3.  Is it appropriate to pray for wealth?
*Yes . . . but motives are critical.

B4.  If "territory" represents relationships, in what ways do you think God might want you to enlarge your personal territory? Why?
*Become more active in serving in church ministries.
*Join a small group.
*Learn how and be willing to share your faith story.
*Reconcile with someone.

## C. BLESSING
C1.  Jabez's first request was to be blessed. Do you think it is appropriate to ask God to bless you?
*Yes.
*It means we are asking God to work in our life for good.
*Blessing means God grants us His favor or grace. It can also mean we receive His goodness. In today's culture, unfortunately, many think it refers to only prosperity or well-being.

C2.  When you ask for blessing what are you personally thinking you are asking for? What are you expecting?
*The Beatitudes of Mt 5:3-12 tell us what the Bible describes as a life worthy of blessing:

*The Beatitudes
"Blessed are the poor in spirit, because the kingdom of heaven is theirs. 4 Blessed are those who mourn, because they will be comforted. 5 Blessed are the gentle, because they will inherit the earth. 6 Blessed are those who hunger and thirst for righteousness, because they will be filled. 7 Blessed are the merciful, because they will be shown mercy. 8 Blessed are the pure in heart, because they will see God. 9 Blessed are the peacemakers, because they

will be called sons of God. 10 Blessed are those who are <u>persecuted for righteousness</u>, because the kingdom of heaven is theirs. 11 "Blessed are you when they <u>insult you and persecute you</u> and falsely say every kind of evil against you <u>because of Me</u>. 12 Be glad and rejoice, because your reward is great in heaven. For that is how they persecuted the prophets who were before you.  HCSB

C3.  How do you think God responds to an "open-ended" honest request for blessing? (An open-ended request means there are no specifics.)
*It's likely God would respond first to His plans for you and after that to your needs.

C4.  What would your life look like if God poured out His blessing on you and your family? In what areas of your life would He be most likely to bless you? Why?
*<u>POSSIBLE AREAS:</u>
*Wealth, so it can be given away or used for ministry.
*Character, such as mercy and empathy to serve others.
*Ministry to serve and help others.
*Relationships to encourage and build up one another.
*Career to provide for needs.
*Spiritual gifts to serve others at a high level.
*Fruit of the Spirit to move us toward perfection.
*Relationship with God so that we truly know Him.
*Guard my lips so I cannot hurt others.
*The Beatitudes.

C5.  Do you think God's blessings are conditional or unconditional?  Why? Why not?
*God does provide unconditional blessing and unconditional love, but many of the promises in the Bible are conditional on some type of behavior on our part. There are many "so that" and "If you will . . I will" statements in Scripture. For example:
> *John 12:36     While you have the light, believe in the light, that you may
> become sons of light. ESV

*Many Biblical promises are conditional, indicating if we do something, then God will do something. For example:
> *1 Peter 5:6    *Humble yourselves, therefore, under the mighty hand of God so that at the proper time he may exalt you. ESV*

   *Q.  Given that many of God's blessings are conditional what do you conclude?
   *My life must be focused.
   *I need to be fully committed.
   *I need to truly abide in Christ.

## D. POWER
D1.  Was there a time in <u>your</u> life when you asked for God's power? What happened?

D2.  What are some of the excuses we all give for staying in our comfort zones?

## Jabez

*LEADER: The following Scriptures speak against the excuse listed.

*SHY

   *2 Tim 1:7; Pr 29:25; Jer 1:6-8; Heb 13:6.

   *2 Tim 1:7   for God gave us a spirit not of fear [NIV says "timidity"] but of power
       and love and self-control. ESV

*NOT GIFTED

   *1 Cor 1:26-29; 2 Cor 4:7, 12:6-7; Ro 12:5-8.

   *1 Cor 1:27   But God chose what is foolish in the world to shame the wise; God chose
       what is weak in the world to shame the strong. ESV

*MIGHT FAIL

   *Mt 10:18-20; Ps 18:28-36; Nahum 1:7.

   *Matt 10:19   When they deliver you over, do not be anxious how you are to speak or
       what you are to say, for what you are to say will be given to you in that hour. ESV

*TRUST or CONTROL

   *Pr 3:5-6; Ps 27:1, 37:3-7, 56:3-4; Heb 11:1, 6; Ro 12:1.

   *Pr 3:5   Trust in the Lord with all your heart, and do not lean on your own understanding.

*TOO BUSY

   *Mt 6:33-34; 11:28-30; Isa 40:29-31; Mk 10:27; Php 4:12-13; Heb 10:35-38

*FEAR

   *Mt 10:28; Heb 13:5-6

## E. EVIL

E1. What evil do you want God to protect you from?  Are there areas of your life that you play close to the edge where you would desire God's power to keep you safe?

*Love of money or wealth.

*Guarding my lips.

*Guarding my eyes (immoral images are everywhere).

E2. If Satan designed a trap or temptation to snare you, what would it be? Or what is your greatest weakness? We are normally vulnerable at our weak points.

*Doubt and fear.

*LEADER: If you get little response from the group, ask, "How could Satan totally destroy your witness?"

     *Adultery.

     *Pornography.

     *Addiction to drugs, alcohol, etc.

     *Pride.

     *Power.

## F. APPLICATION

F1. What, if anything, are you doing today that requires God's power, other than life in general?

F2.  Do you have not because you ask not? Does your prayer life need to improve and become more focused?

F3.  Are you asking for the things you need or for what you want?

F4.  Do your prayers have eternal significance? For example, do you pray:

>That my life would bring praise and honor to God.
>
>That I would know God.
>
>That I have a right relationship with Christ.
>
>That my worship is acceptable and heartfelt.
>
>That I thirst for the truth of God's Word.
>
>That I love God with all my heart, strength, mind, soul.
>
>That Christ is the central focus and reality of my life.
>
>That I always have a thankful heart.

F5.  Are your prayers big enough?

*Probably not!

*Q.  What big thing are you <u>not</u> praying for that seems too extravagant, or beyond your reach?

>**\*LEADER:** You could stop the group discussion here and pray for a few of these desires.

## Challenge Exercise:

"Bless Me": *Lord, I desire Your blessing! Please pour out in my life every possible blessing You desire for me. Father, I want You working in my life and I need the guidance and direction of the Holy Spirit so that my walk is pleasing to You. Bless me so that I can be a blessing to others. I desire Your blessing so that You receive honor and thanksgiving from others who see You working in my life.*

*Bless me O Lord.  AMEN.*

Q.  When you read the above what strikes you?  What do you notice about this prayer?
>*It is about what God wants, not what I want.
>
>*It is about being a blessing to God and others.
>
>*It is not focused on self.

*"Expand My Territory"
>*WHY: So I can bring glory to God, and bless others.

*"Put Your Hand Upon Me"
>*WHY: I can't do it myself, I need His help.

*"Protect Me From Evil"
>*WHY: The struggle is against spiritual forces of evil. (Eph 6:2)

*"Help Me Not Cause Pain"
>*WHY: Life is tough. It is easy to offend or injure. Guard my ways.

"John Wesley believed that God does nothing except in answer to prayer, so if we are to accomplish anything of eternal value, we must do it from our knees."

Dr. Terry Teykl[8]

# The OBSCURE Bible Study Series

*Grow in your faith through examining fascinating and unusual biblical stories and events.*

**WEBSITE:**  http://getwisdompublishing.com/products/

**AMAZON:**  www.amazon.com/author/stephenhberkey

## Unique, new, and fresh

This unique series uses a number of lesser-known Bible characters and events to explore such major themes as Angels, being Born Again, Courage, Death, Evangelism, Faithfulness, Forgiveness, Grace, Hell, Leadership, Miracles, the Remnant, the Sabbath, Salvation, Rebellion, Sovereignty, Thankfulness, Women, the World, Creation, and End Times.

The series as a whole provides both a broad and fresh understanding of the nature of God as we see Him act in the lives of people we've never examined before.

Most of the people chosen for these studies are unfamiliar because they are mentioned only a few times in Scripture – fifteen only once or twice. Others, although more familiar, are included because of their particular contribution to kingdom work.

For example, Scripture mentions Shamgar only twice. One verse in Judges 3:31 tells his story and 5:6 simply establishes a timeline and says nothing more about him. Then there is Nicodemus, with whom we associate the concept of being "born again." His name appears only 5 times, all in one short passage in the book of John. Eve, although obviously not obscure, is included in order to investigate the creation story.

## Knowledge of Scripture

These studies are a great introduction for those just beginning Bible study. Regardless of their level of knowledge, everyone should find the characters and stories provide an opportunity to grow their faith through investigating fascinating and unusual biblical stories and incidents.

## Valuable life lessons

These lesser-known characters are a lot like you and me. God uses all sorts of people to accomplish His plans! You will become familiar with ordinary people, strange characters, and people living on the fringe of life who have troubles and challenges just as people today. The deep truths and life lessons embedded in these studies will be valuable in providing new insights to scripture.

## Group discussion or individual study

These studies can be done individually or in a small discussion group. The real value of the study is in the discussion questions. We all see life differently and the thoughts and ideas shared in a group will lead to a richer understanding of the Scripture. The questions often require the participant to put himself (herself) in the mind or circumstances of that person in the Scriptures.

## Ideal For both new and mature bible students

The commentary portion of the introductory material in each lesson will clarify the passage and set the stage for the discussion questions. The questions are designed to help the student understand the meaning of the text itself and explore the kingdom implications from a personal point of view.

The lessons have three underlying questions:

- "Who is this person?"
- "What is happening here?"
- "What is the implication for my life?"

Because of the obscurity of the characters under study, chances are that even experienced participants with prior understanding of the lesson's theme will find fresh material to explore.

## Extensive Leader Guide

All of the books in the Bible Study series have an extensive Leader Guide. If you are a participant in a group, a Leader Guide is not necessary, unless you want the author's answers. If you are studying independently, you may want the Leader Guide.

The Guide is designed to give the small group leader more than enough information to effectively lead a discussion of each lesson. It contains additional information and background as well as follow-up questions that might be asked.

You do not need to be a Bible student, a mature Christian, or knowledgeable about the Bible to lead a group discussion with this Guide.

All you need is a desire and basic group facilitating skills. No outside study or research is required. You simply need to read the questions aloud and keep the group discussion on target.

## Benefits and summary

- This is the story of the Bible and the Gospel presented in a new, interesting, and fresh setting.

- These ordinary believers, strange characters, and lesser-known individuals have the same troubles and circumstances as people today.

- This is a unique approach to bible study – fun, unique, but meaningful.

- You will learn timeless truths in a different and revealing way.

- The OBSCURE Series provides new insights to life and Scripture.

# The OBSCURE Bible Study Series

**WEBSITE:**  http://getwisdompublishing.com/products/

**AMAZON:**  www.amazon.com/author/stephenhberkey

### Meet Shamgar, Jethro, Manoah & Hathach
**An introduction to the OBSCURE Bible Study Series.**

This book of four lessons is provided at a reduced cost so that students and leaders can get a first-hand experience and introduction to The *OBSCURE* Bible Study Series.

### Blasphemy, Grace, Quarrels & Reconciliation
**The intriguing lives of first-century disciples.**

This book presents Joseph of Arimathea, Joanna, Ananias, Hymenaeus, and Cornelius (a centurion). It illustrates the nature and challenges of life as a first-century disciple. Life has real challenges, but they can be overcome.

### The Beginning and the End
**From creation to eternity.**

This book has four lessons from Genesis and four from the book of Revelation. It covers such topics as creation, rebellion, grace, worship, and eternity. It illustrates how God is leading us to worship in the Throne Room.

### God at the Center
**He is sovereign and I am not.**

This book examines the virgin birth, worship, prayer, the sovereignty of God, compromise, and trust. God is at the center of all these stories. He is there in the shadows or openly orchestrating our lives. Regardless of the situation He is at the center of our lives – a sovereign almighty God.

## Women of Courage
### God did some serious business with these women.

This book examines the lives of Jael, Rizpah, the woman of Tekoa, Tabitha, Shiphrah, and Lydia. We see these women exhibiting great courage and faithfulness. God used them in amazing ways and we can use their example for encouragement and spiritual leadership.

## The Beginning of Wisdom
### Your personal character counts.

In this book we find courage, loyalty, thankfulness, love, forgiveness, and humility. Personal character counts. It is critical to make good decisions because they have consequences. Building our lives on wisdom will help us stand firm in our faith. We should reject the example of Demas who deserted Paul for the values of the world.

## Miracles & Rebellion
### The good, the bad, and the indifferent.

This book contrasts characters who rebelled against God with those who trusted in Him. God hates sin and loves to heal the faithful. The rebellion of Korah, Haman, and Alexander are included to compare with the healing stories of Aeneas, a slave girl, and the crippled man at Lystra.

## The Chosen People
### There is a remnant.

This book concentrates mostly on Israel in the Old Testament, but also covers some interesting subjects as Lucifer, Michael the archangel, and Job's wife.

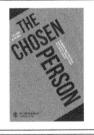

## The Chosen Person
### Keep your eyes on Jesus.

The focus of this book is on Jesus and the superiority of Christ. We investigate Melchizedek, the disciples on the road to Emmaus, Nicodemus, the criminal on the cross who asks to be remembered by Jesus, and others.

**WEBSITE:**   http://getwisdompublishing.com/products/

**AMAZON:**   www.amazon.com/author/stephenhberkey

# Acknowledgments

### *Arlene*
Arlene has served as wife, editor, and proof-reader for all of my writing – thank you for your patience, help, and love.

### *Michelle*
Michelle, our older daughter, has been an invaluable resource. She has graciously produced the website at www.getwisdompublishing.com. She was the first author in the family: graceandthegravelroad.com.

### *Stephanie*
Our middle daughter designed all the covers for the *OBSCURE* Bible Study Series, as well as the marks and logos for Get Wisdom Publishing. She also designed the cover for this book. We are grateful for her help, talent and creativity.

### *God, Jesus, and Holy Spirit*
Thank you, Lord, for Your guidance and direction.

# Notes

1 *Purpose in Prayer*, E. M. Bounds, Baker Book House, Grand Rapids MI, (New Edition), Copyright 1991 by Baker Book House Company, ISBN: 0-8010-1010-1, page 11.

2 *Purpose in Prayer*, E. M. Bounds, Baker Book House, Grand Rapids MI, (New Edition), Copyright 1991 by Baker Book House Company, ISBN: 0-8010-1010-1.

3 *Prayer the Great Adventure*, David Jeremiah, Multnomah Publishers, Sisters Oregon, copyright 1977, page 69.

4 *Handle With Prayer*, Charles Stanley, Victor Books, Wheaton IL, ISBN 0-89693-963-4, page 10.

5 *Lord Teach Me to Pray*, Kay Arthur, Harvest House Publishers, Eugene Oregon, copyright 1982/2008, page 104.

6 *Let Prayer Change Your Life*, Becky Tirabassi, Thomas Nelson Publishers, Nashville, copyright 1990, page 9.

7 *Too Busy Not to Pray*, Bill Hybels, InterVarsity Press, Downers Grove IL, copyright 1988, page 62.

8 *Pray the Price*, Dr. Terry Teykl, Prayer Point Press, copyright 1997, page 17.

# About the Author

Steve attended church as a child and accepted Christ when he was 10 years old. But his walk with Jesus left a lot to be desired for the next 44 years. In 1994 he "wrestled" with God for some period of months and in September of that year totally surrendered his life to Jesus.

In 1996 he attended the Indianapolis campus of Trinity Evangelical Divinity School (Chicago) to earn a Certificate of Biblical Studies. His hunger for God's Word led him to write and lead his own Bible studies for his small group. He has been an entrepreneur and Bible study leader for the past 25 years.

In 2019 he was one of four members who founded The Acanthus Group (www.theacanthusgroup.org). He is a member of The Church at Station Hill in Spring Hill, TN, a regional campus of Brentwood Baptist (Brentwood TN).

In 2020 he founded Get Wisdom Publishing in order to publish *The OBSCURE Bible Study Series*, a group of nine books (68 lessons) focused on obscure characters and events in the Bible. This Prayer Guide includes the complete lesson on "The Prayer of Jebez," with the answers to the discussion questions at the end. You can find more information about the *OBSCURE* Series at:

**WEBSITE:**   http://getwisdompublishing.com/

**AMAZON:**   www.amazon.com/author/stephenhberkey

# Contact Us

**Website:**       www.getwisdompublishing.com

**Email:**       info@getwisdompublishing.com

**Facebook:**       Get Wisdom Publishing

**Author's Page:**     www.amazon.com/author/stephenhberkey

**Resources:**

### *Get Wisdom – Resources:*
You can access free resources from Get Wisdom by going to:

**www.getwisdom.link/resources**

### *You can help:*

IDEAS and SUGGESTIONS: If you have a suggestion on how the *Prayer Guide* could be improved and made more useful, please let us know.

Mention the *Prayer Guide* on your social platforms.

Recommend the *Prayer Guide* to your family, friends, small group or Sunday School class, or anyone who prays.

*Thank you!*

Made in the USA
Middletown, DE
04 May 2021